The Credible Trainer

Create Value
for Training,
Get Respect
for Your Ideas,
and Boost
Your Career

D1399700

ASTD

*Linking People,
Learning & Performance*

Robert J. Rosania

Ordering information: Books published by ASTD can be ordered by calling 800.628.2783 or 703.683.8100, or via the Website at www.astd.org.

Library of Congress Catalog Card Number: 00-109203

ISBN: 1-56286-145-X

Contents

Preface

This book is a way to share the many lessons I have learned in my two decades as a trainer with you who share my love and respect for the field of training. I have chosen not to focus on the skills and techniques involved in designing and producing training activities. Rather, this book will help you design a strategic approach to developing your training career. I will introduce you to some new ways of thinking and acting that will help you build trust and establish your credibility with your clients, customers, and peers. In turn, you will learn to use your credibility as a trainer as a positive force for influencing outcomes that will help you move your organization toward its goals.

This book consists of 11 chapters; each concludes with a self-assessment exercise that suggests various action items to help you become a credible trainer. In chapter 1, I introduce the key to success for all trainers—establishing your credibility. In chapters 2 through 4, I present three factors to help you achieve this goal. Chapters 5 through 7 introduce three important elements for creating an organizational environment that will be supportive of and responsive to the needs of employees and their development. In chapter 8, I present a discussion of the tactical side of training. Returning to strategy in chapter 9, I introduce an effective approach for becoming a training leader, followed by chapter 10, which examines the future of training. In chapter 11, I offer an opportunity for you to begin planning your own professional development and taking charge of your career.

This book is geared for a wide audience of new practitioners and veteran trainers alike. Naturally, some suggestions are more appropriate for trainers at one end or the other of the experience spectrum. For example, if you are new to the field or report to a training manager, it may be wise to check with your immediate supervisor before acting on some of the suggestions offered in the book. Although some suggestions may not be suitable for use right now, they will likely provide direction and serve as a source of ideas for the future as you continue to build your credibility.

It is with love that I dedicate this book to my son, Aaron. I gratefully acknowledge my wife, Vera Regoli, for her unconditional love and support, which has had as much to do with the completion of this book as any words I have written. Profound thanks are due to my loving parents, Al and Louise Rosania, for all of life's lessons they have taught me. Special thanks to Skip Lange for sharing his wisdom and for his unwavering support. John Brady provided expert help on chapter 3 for which I am most grateful. Finally, I thank Angela McGlynn for her friendship, encouragement, and love over all these years.

Robert J. Rosania
January 2001

Introduction

I remember my first day on the job as a trainer when I became a training specialist at a large New York City hospital. After working for six years in higher education as a counselor and administrator, I had decided to make a career change and was ready for the chance to start a dream job in my new profession.

I hopped on the train in New Jersey and two hours, two subway stations, and a six-block walk later, found myself standing in front of a high-rise apartment building that housed my new office. As I looked around at the huge hospital complex, I was overtaken with an adrenaline rush, fueled with anticipation and excitement. After all, my new boss had told me that I had been selected from more than 100 job applicants. Brimming with confidence, I entered the building and took the elevator to the training office on the fourth floor. As I opened the door to the office, I was ready to make the most of this opportunity. I was going to be the best trainer they ever hired!

Well, that happened more than 20 years ago. My "dream" job at the hospital ended in a nightmare only nine months later because of a large layoff. As for being the best trainer the hospital ever had, no plaque attesting to that distinction hangs on the wall of my office (or any place else). I went on to work at two more hospitals in those early years. Like so many other new trainers, I spent much time feeling humbled, not only by my lack of expertise but by my inability to influence any of those organizations in ways that would help them grow and succeed. I struggled with the challenge of establishing credibility while working in a function traditionally viewed as having little power in setting strategy and achieving bottom-line results. I began to doubt whether I could indeed make a difference.

I am not sure when my epiphany occurred. After leaving the health-care industry and entering the service management field, I noticed that some trainers were able to create their own opportunities and spread their influence throughout the organization. Often these trainers positioned themselves on the right committee or established a relationship with a key vice president. The proposals of those trainers were the ones that were accepted; those trainers were the ones who were able to secure funding for projects. They were purposeful in their actions and behaved in a way that demonstrated that they knew what they wanted to achieve and, even more important, had a plan to get there.

What always impressed me was their strategic thinking; they acted and made decisions based on what made most sense for their organization's future. Although I did not realize it at the time, what they had is commonly referred to today as emotional intelligence. They saw the big picture and understood the value they brought to their organizations. What set them apart from others, though, was their ability to articulate a plan for achieving their own goals and the goals of their organizations. What they had was credibility, that quality that inspired others to believe in them. I realized that only by working to establish my own credibility could I hope to develop into a training professional who could influence the direction of my organization and help it grow, prosper, and achieve its goals.

I learned to think and act strategically from more experienced colleagues. I started with little things, such as attaching handwritten notes to articles and books that I had read on hot topics and then sending them to important people in the organization. I discovered that when I hit on something that caught a major player's eye, I would be included in discussions with people who suddenly were interested in my expertise and what I had to say.

I realized that I was less apt to be taken seriously during discussions with influential people in the organization if I lacked knowledge about company finances and sources of income. I was at a still greater disadvantage when it came time to explain how training contributed to bottom-line results. This lack of knowledge left large cracks in my credibility. To begin sealing these cracks, I took a course on finance for nonfinancial managers.

I saw that successful trainers were able to relate their training directly to pressing business needs and issues confronting their organizations. Because they understood their organizations, they were able to sell their ideas about training to decision makers in the company and related as peers to those who attended their sessions. They had credibility because they understood that to be better trainers they had to venture out of their offices and spend time in the field learning about the organization from the bottom up.

As my career has progressed, I have learned from my valued role models that my behavior and how it is perceived by clients, customers, and peers plays a critical part in my success as a trainer and leader. Those I have watched and learned from often display an air of professionalism that goes beyond appearance and charisma. They pay attention to the little details, such as personally connecting with every person who enters their training or meeting room. By taking the initiative to introduce themselves first, they remove any barriers that might normally exist between teacher and student or line workers and staff, allowing relationships to develop based on trust and respect. I have learned from watching others and experiencing myself that actions truly do speak louder than words when trying to influence people to your way of thinking.

About six years ago I left the corporate world and joined a small consulting firm dedicated to helping organizations achieve results through their people. Five years later I decided to venture out on my own. Today my success is measured in ways most often determined by my clients. I, though, measure my success in more demanding terms. I can prosper only if my credibility remains intact; I can succeed only if I continually prove myself worthy of my clients' trust and respect.

As you read this book, you will find that your effectiveness as a trainer is measured not so much by what you do but rather by the accomplishments of the people whom you train and influence. To achieve the right outcomes takes a special person who not only has the knowledge and skill to affect the thinking and actions of people, but who also has the credibility to influence the direction of an entire organization. This book is dedicated to helping you become that special person.

1

The Key to Success: Establishing Your Credibility

"You may know someone is clearly competent, dynamic, and inspirational. But, if you have a sense that that person is not being honest, you will not accept the message, and you will not willingly follow. So the credibility check can reliably be simplified to just one question: 'Do I trust this person?'" (Kouzes & Posner, 1995a).

 CHANGE YOUR THINKING ABOUT HOW YOU CAN BUILD CREDIBILITY, THINK STRATEGICALLY, AND CONTRIBUTE TO THE SUCCESS OF YOUR ORGANIZATION.

What is it about the training profession that draws so many people from fields as diverse as social work, teaching, marketing, as well as from operations or staff positions in every conceivable industry you can think of? Many experienced trainers, those who have been working in the field for at least 10 years, often point to their own participation in a training program or workshop in their workplace or community as their first real exposure to the profession. For many, this experience often provided a first glimpse of a different world where people can make a living by mixing learning and business.

Today many trainers, perhaps most, still come to the field by way of other professions, but many new practitioners now are able to take advantage of new approaches and accompanying best practices that help adults learn more effectively. Pioneers in the field—people like William Rothwell, Jim Fuller, and Jim and Dana Robinson, to name a few—have introduced fresh ways of thinking that are helping redefine the field. People interested in becoming trainers can now study about training and development through college and graduate programs popping up around the country, programs that were still in their infancy in the late eighties and early nineties. Unlike their older colleagues who learned as they went along, those new to the profession now have a distinct advantage of working in a field that is growing and maturing every day. Today when you walk into a local bookstore or go online, it is not unusual to see numerous books devoted to educating new trainers and exploring new training approaches, such as action learning and performance consulting. As this book will show, however, as much as things change, they also stay the same. Despite the new approaches that are available for training, many trainers are still mired in the same old way of doing things. This book is devoted to helping trainers think differently about their approach to what they do and create more value in their organization.

TOUCHING PEOPLE'S HEARTS AND MINDS

One way to understand why old habits die hard is to look at why trainers become trainers in the first place. One reason expressed countless times by many in the profession is that training truly offers the potential to touch the hearts and minds of those people they serve. Training equips people with the means to help improve work performance and productivity in an atmosphere that encourages playing games, brainstorming ideas, watching videos made by such people as ex-Monty Python player John Cleese, and even having fun. Trainers are in a unique position, because they can positively affect an entire organization's culture by simply exposing people to new skills, new ways of thinking, and new ways of doing their work.

POWER TO INFLUENCE

The trainer's ability to influence an organization directly might seem a contradictory concept to most trainers. Trainers have long lamented their lack of power within their organizations and their inability to gain access to those who have power. If you look a little closer, though, much of this feeling of powerlessness is self-inflicted. It may be true that in most organizations trainers are rarely accorded the status of some of their colleagues in terms of title or department affiliation. You will have to look for awhile—a long while—before you find someone working in an organization with the title of vice president of training. It happens, but not very often. It is true that trainers have customarily been assigned to the organization's HR department, an area that has traditionally played second fiddle to other support areas such as finance, sales, and marketing.

The fact is that trainers do not inherently lack power; what they lack is the ability to use their power in a way that consistently demonstrates the value of their service to their stakeholders. Trainers do not need fancy titles or affiliation with certain departments to demonstrate their value. What trainers need to change is their thinking about how they can contribute to the success of their organizations.

Too often trainers have been satisfied operating on the periphery. Instead of participating in their organization's business, learning about it, and understanding its goals, trainers have often reverted to the comfort of the training or HR department. When this happens, the value trainers bring to their organization diminishes as they get bogged down doing training-related tasks, rather than focusing on the goals of the organization. Although it is important to devote time and energy to training programs, it is even more important to ask whether the programs are designed to help the organization achieve its goals. Is it any wonder, then, that trainers who take a purely tactical approach to their work are often not taken seriously by those they are there to serve?

THE MEANING OF POWER FOR TRAINERS

The power that you as a trainer can achieve has nothing to do with manipulating people so that they will do what you want them to do. That kind of power is negative and destructive. The power to influence is more subtle and ultimately more powerful. The training enterprise can truly make a difference as it helps move a company toward its stated mission and goals. Trainers who take a straight tactical approach to providing services limit their power to influence and provide fewer opportunities for the organization to grow and its people to succeed. A classic example of wasting the power to influence is reacting to the person who seems to be shouting the loudest without asking if the training they want is necessary and whether it will help the organization achieve its strategic goals. Without such questioning, trainers lose the opportunity to create a positive influence and demonstrate their value to the organization.

ESTABLISH YOUR CREDIBILITY

Of course, having the power to influence an organization's direction does not come automatically with your appointment as a trainer in the training department. Cynical trainers may chuckle at the thought and say it works in just the opposite way: that the power to influence the organization falls when you become a trainer. That is the point. If you believe you have no power to influence in your organization, then you have no power. Such power must be earned, and the first step in this process is to establish your credibility.

What exactly is credibility? *Webster's* defines it as the quality or power of inspiring belief. Simply stated, you have credibility when people trust you and believe you to be truthful and honest in doing what you say you will do. As you can imagine, establishing your credibility with people in your organization takes time. Whether you are a new practitioner, a seasoned professional new to your organization, or someone who has worked in an organization for some time, credibility is about building relationships based on trust and respect, as well as demonstrating to others your understanding of the organization and its culture.

Why is establishing your credibility as a trainer so important? Once again, it goes back to the issue of your ability to use your power to influence. Think of it this way: You have a race car with state-of-the-art equipment so that it can go 200 miles per hour, but it has no steering wheel. You may have the power to get the car moving fast, but you will end up all over the track. Your credibility is your steering wheel, which represents your ability to use all the power that comes from your position as a trainer to help guide your organization in the direction that it needs to go. Like the fancy equipment on the race car, your repertoire of skills, techniques, and knowledge is important but is secondary to how credible you are in the eyes of those people you are serving. If people do not have confidence in you and believe your words, it really does not make much difference how proficiently you present a workshop or program or how much you know about the subject. But, your audience—your customers—expects more from you than just good form and technique. Although they certainly expect you to be articulate and hold their attention as you communicate with them either in a group or individually, what they really want is to trust you and believe what you say. They need to know that when you speak, you are representing exactly what they need to know to be successful in their organization. When you establish your credibility with those you serve, then and only then are you in a position to exert your power to influence in a positive and meaningful way.

CREDIBILITY IS DIRECTLY RELATED TO SUCCESS

A trainer, simply as a function of his or her role, is often placed in a position of authority to carry the messages the organization wishes to have disseminated to its employees. This situation carries an awesome responsibility because the trainer is in a position to exert great power to influence. These messages come in many forms: introducing new skills employees will use to perform their work, enacting higher standards for meeting customer expectations, and defining acceptable ways of acting and behaving. In many ways these messages, both direct and indirect, help set the tone for the organization and become a part of its culture. Because these messages are critical to the success of the organization, it is easy to see why they must come from someone who has integrity and the respect of those who are receiving them. Can you imagine an organization sending forth a messenger who is to influence the thinking and performance of its people yet who is not credible?

Unfortunately this situation arises. For example, one service provider organization had decided to do business using TQM principles. The idea was a good one: Keep and attract new clients by transforming the organization into one in which quality comes first. A very popular national TQM supplier was chosen, and the organization set out to change the ways all its employees—front-line workers to senior executives—were to be educated about the tenets of TQM and trained in the skills and techniques to implement this new approach. Internal HR professionals and regional managers were trained to deliver the training to the rest of the company using materials and videos, some of which were customized to make them more relevant to the organization. The extensive training effort was instituted with a great deal of fanfare, and the implementation required more than a year.

You can probably guess what happened. It did not work, not because the training materials were of poor quality or because the level of training was deficient, but because there was not complete buy-in at all organizational levels to the goals of being a quality organization. Not even the trainers, who were the ones responsible for imparting the TQM tenets, completely supported what they were teaching the employees. As this wavering commitment became exposed within the organization, the trainers' credibility eroded as their message became less and less believable. Although the company spent more than a million dollars on this well-intentioned effort, no lasting effect of the intensive training was apparent in the day-to-day activities of the managers or the employees. Without a credible message expressed by credible messengers, this effort was doomed from the beginning.

ALL THINGS TO ALL PEOPLE

Too often trainers get caught up in the notion that they must be all things to all people, and this false belief sometimes jeopardizes their credibility in their organizations. Perhaps this is derived from some altruistic bent, but it often results in a trainer being pulled in many different directions at the expense of the work he or she is doing. Once again, this usually occurs when a trainer takes a purely tactical, rather than strategic, approach to providing service to his or her organization and its people. The trainer's credibility then becomes a hit-or-miss proposition, depending on which customers are being served and the issue being addressed. For example, if you drop everything to conduct a series of stress management workshops for the vice president of finance's staff of 50 people, you may gain stature in the vice president's mind, but you may lose credibility with others who perceive that you were diverted from activities that were better aligned with the organization's goals.

Trainers, it seems, have been programmed over the years to never say no—an affliction that has done them and their organizations more harm than good. It is easy to see how you can lose your credibility when this happens, especially if you are only known for being the person who conducts training programs in the organization. You have probably heard many "training" requests that sound like this one: "I need a program on leadership, but we only have one day, and some of my people are going to have to leave an hour early. Oh, and another thing, you need to make sure that it's fun." Think about the number of times you have found yourself in no-win situations, when you are asked to perform work that simply does not make sense, but you give in anyway. This kind of reactive response is what often gets trainers in trouble and is a surefire way of losing credibility in your organization.

TO BE CREDIBLE MEANS BEING COMPETENT

Obviously there is more to establishing credibility than just having a strategic approach to your work. To be credible means you also must be competent to perform the training services you provide. Competence, or the perception of competence, is an important issue for individuals coming from an operations or a staff position who are now expected to be trainers. Although they may be deemed competent as front-line managers or salespeople, this perceived competence does not transfer automatically to their new training positions. The perception of competence is also a factor in the success of new practitioners and even seasoned professionals. "Is this person capable of helping my department and the organization work more effectively?" may run through the mind of a manager or employee when determining whether to use a trainer's service on an issue or project. This thinking becomes even more important when previous experience with training professionals or the department in general has been negative. Then the question becomes one of trust: "Why should I believe that this person will be any more helpful than the others?" As you can see, there is more to being a successful trainer than just knowing how to write or present a program and knowing how to operate the overhead projector.

Your competence is judged in many ways that range from the way you assess your customer's needs to the training intervention you design and implement to the way you conduct yourself before your customers. However, the most critical factor in how your competence is judged boils down to one thing: Has the performance of those affected by your training intervention improved? The perception of competence is subjective, especially when the evaluation is conducted by people who are not experts themselves on effective training. They are experts, though, in gauging your bottom-line effectiveness: whether their productivity or their department's productivity improved after the training or whether the performance of those involved in the training improved.

This means that your competence is measured more by the results you help generate and less about your technical proficiency. What is interesting is that this is somewhat contrary to the way trainers and training are normally evaluated. For example, the familiar smile sheets that are distributed to an audience after a training session normally measure satisfaction with the process of training and the skill level of the trainer. Even if they attempt to deal with an individual's level of performance or productivity after the session as compared with before, mostly this is done in the form of a self-evaluation through evaluation items like this: "Please evaluate your ability to use active listening skills before this program using a scale of 1–5," followed by a question asking the participant about his or her ability to use skills after the program. Usually if the program is well constructed and the trainer competently delivers the material (and the hotel has great food and a nice swimming pool), most people will indicate that the program was good, that the trainer did a fine job, and that their skill level as an active listener improved.

What happens in the classroom is not necessarily a good indicator of what will happen outside the classroom. This statement, by no means, implies that conducting training programs is a waste of time. What it suggests is that the traditional role of the trainer as the person who only conducts training programs is quickly becoming obsolete. Why? First, it is difficult to ensure the transfer of learning outside the classroom and, second, because fundamental problems complicate the measurement of trainee success. Now, take this premise one step further and look at it from a trainer's perspective. If your success is based on the results of your trainees' performance after they leave your classroom and if competence is a critical component in your credibility, then you need to seek appropriate opportunities to provide services to your customers in ways that extend beyond traditional approaches. Even taking the trainer out of the equation, most trainers know that traditional classroom training cannot guarantee improvement in participant performance. This book explores some alternative approaches that trainers can use to provide their services outside of the classroom.

HOW DO YOU BEGIN TO ESTABLISH YOUR CREDIBILITY?

How do you begin to establish your credibility? Although the methods differ, depending on whether you are a new practitioner or someone who has been a trainer for years, some elements of establishing your credibility apply in all situations. In many ways, if you are someone who is new to the profession, you have an advantage simply because you get to start with a clean slate. Of course, as is always the case, there is a downside. Because you are a new trainer, your credibility automatically is minimal. Even seasoned professionals do not necessarily get a free pass on this issue. With the dramatic changes going on in and outside of the business world, the old adage, "What have you done for me lately?" still applies. Your customers want to know that when you offer a suggestion or recommendation about a training-related issue that what you are providing is based on the most up-to-date information, not the same old programmed approach.

To a great extent, credibility is in the eye of many beholders. It is common to find yourself disagreeing with someone on the issue of another person's credibility. The world of politics and business offers many examples of this. If your success as a trainer and the success of your organization depend on your ability to be perceived as someone who is trusted and believable, then it stands to reason that you need to do whatever it takes to positively influence this perception.

THREE KEY FACTORS

Several factors affect how effectively you build credibility within your organization. The three most important factors are the following:

- Remember that people judge you by your behavior and the way you act toward others.
- Know your business and its strategic goals.
- Understand your organization's culture.

New practitioners and seasoned professionals must remember that actions speak louder than words. As we go about developing relationships within our organizations, we make impressions with those around us by how we act in various situations. People judge you by your behavior and the way you act toward others. Are your actions in alignment with your words? Do you deliver what you promise? Think of it this way: Everything you do matters—you are always one misstep away from losing your credibility.

The second factor has to do with your ability to know your business and its strategic goals, determine what the organization's people need to be able to do to achieve the goals of the organization, and implement appropriate training interventions to meet those needs. Trainers know the importance of knowledge in their work, and they dedicate a good deal of time to helping others acquire knowledge about concepts and ideas in order to make better decisions about what they should do. It is important that you are perceived as being technically competent, that is, knowledgeable about designing, developing, and implementing training interventions to meet the needs of your organization. But, it is a mistake to increase your knowledge of the training field at the expense of other types of knowledge, especially knowledge about your business and its strategic goals. If you cannot state specifically what it is your organization is in business to do, what its strategic goals are, what plan is in place to achieve them, and what your role as a trainer is in making this all happen, chances are you may be lacking the credibility necessary to make a difference.

The third factor has to do with your organization's culture. You need to understand what makes your organization tick. What are the values that determine how your organization conducts business? Who are the heroes, present and past, who shape the direction your organization is headed? What are the acceptable behaviors in your organization? These are some of the questions that you must be able to answer to establish your credibility as a trainer in your organization.

The chapter 1 self-assessment will help you picture the credible trainer you want to be and the changes you must make to become this person. What immediate actions can you take to make this picture a reality?

The next chapter will open with an exploration of the ways trainers establish their credibility through their behavior, actions, and relationships with others.

Self-Assessment 1-1.
Establishing your credibility in your organization.

On a scale of 1 to 10, rate yourself on the three key factors for building credibility in your organization by circling the appropriate number on the numbered scale.

Key Factor 1: Remember that people judge you by your behavior and the way you act toward others.

1. My actions are in alignment with my words.

Never				Sometimes				Always	
1	2	3	4	5	6	7	8	(9)	10

2. What kind of impression do I make on those with whom I work?

Poor				Average				Star performer	
1	2	3	4	5	6	7	8	9	(10)

3. Do I deliver what I promise?

Rarely				Sometimes				Always	
1	2	3	4	5	6	7	8	9	(10)

4. I would rate my credibility in the organization as:

Not credible				Somewhat credible				Very credible	
1	2	3	4	5	6	7	8	9	(10)

Action Items

If you scored yourself 7 or below on any of the items relating to the first key factor, think about what you need to change to alter the perception others have of your behaviors, actions, and relationships. Thinking in terms of those you work with, list some actions you can take to begin this process.

☐ Action to take with my immediate supervisor: _____
☐ Action to take with those I manage directly: _____
☐ Action to take with my training peers: _____
☐ Action to take with my customers: _____

Key Factor 2: Know your business and its strategic goals.

5. How well do I know my organization's strategic and business goals?

Not at all			Somewhat familiar					Very knowledgeable	
1	2	(3)	4	5	6	7	8	9	10

6. How thoroughly do I determine what the learners need to be able to do to achieve the organization's goals?

Haphazard approach				Somewhat careful				Very thorough	
1	2	3	4	5	6	(7)	8	9	10

continued on page 10

Self-Assessment 1-1.
Establishing your credibility in your organization (continued).

7. How effectively do I design, develop, and implement appropriate interventions to meet learners' needs?

Ineffective				Somewhat effective				Very effective	
1	2	3	4	5	6	7	8	(9)	10

Action Items

What knowledge, information, and competencies do I need to build my credibility in the organization? In terms of the knowledge needed, what immediate actions can I take to acquire them?

☑ Action to take to gain knowledge of my organization's business: _____

☑ Action to take to learn my organization's strategic goals: _____

☐ Action to take to become aware of what the learners need to know to meet the organization's goals: _____

☐ Action to take to become more knowledgeable about designing, developing, and implementing training interventions to meet the needs of your organization:

_____

Key Factor 3: Understand your organization's culture.

8. How readily can I identify the organizational values that determine how it conducts business?

Don't know				Know some values				Can identify many values	
1	2	3	4	(5)	6	7	8	9	10

9. Who are the heroes, present and past, who shape the direction my organization is heading?

Good question!				Can list a name or two				Can readily list several heroes	
1	(2)	3	4	5	6	7	8	9	10

10. What are the acceptable behaviors in my organization?

Don't know				Have some ideas				Clearly familiar with acceptable behaviors	
1	2	(3)	4	5	6	7	8	9	10

Action Items

What organizational practices within my sphere of influence need to be changed so that the training enterprise can gain credibility? What actions can I take immediately to begin this process?

☐ Action to take regarding practices of the training or HR department:

_____

☐ Action to take regarding practices at managerial levels:

_____

☐ Action to take regarding practices in other organizational functions (list):

_____

2

Acting Strategically to Achieve Organizational Goals

"Strategic thinking, after all, is a process of educated guesswork. It is neither all science nor all art; maybe it's a scientific art, or maybe it's an artistic science. There is no divinely inspired truth to be discovered in charting the destiny of any enterprise. There is only the most enlightened concept for success that is possible given the information, energy, and talent applied to the issues" (Albrecht, 1994).

 REMEMBER THAT PEOPLE JUDGE YOU BY YOUR BEHAVIOR AND THE WAY YOU ACT TOWARD OTHERS.

The first key factor for establishing your credibility and building your success as a trainer has to do with your behavior and actions and how they are perceived by others in your organization. Your behavior refers to your personal conduct and comportment—the way you carry yourself. Because everyone is different, no one way of behaving is the right way, but how you act as a trainer is important for several reasons. Remember that you have the power to influence others. For you to successfully use this power you need to act in a way that commands respect and instills confidence in your customers that you know what you are doing. Just as important, you must behave in a way that shows your customers that you are part of their team and not someone whose commitment to their success lasts only from assignment to assignment. How can a trainer accomplish all this and not be pulled in many different directions?

The answer is to think and act strategically, becoming a *strategic trainer*. What, exactly, is the meaning of strategy? Strategy refers to how you get something accomplished. Most organizations have a strategy to manage and grow their business to achieve their mission and goals. Each business unit then develops its own strategy aligned with the organization's and, when working optimally, everyone performs in a manner that helps carry out the strategy. Of course, this does not always work exactly as planned, often because the organization's strategy is not well defined or effectively communicated, or because each person's role in carrying it out is not clarified.

This latter point has always presented a real dilemma for trainers because of their critical role in helping carry out their organization's strategy. Some resourceful trainers have taken things into their own hands by devising their own training strategy based on what they perceive to be their organization's needs and have developed programs and workshops to fill the void. Others have simply reverted back to doing the things they enjoy and do best, offering the same training courses they have been running for years. Although well intentioned, at least from the perspective of doing something, neither of these options is very good.

How then can you become a strategic trainer and be a part of helping your organization grow and achieve its goals? Here are four actions you can put into practice that will help you to act and perform more strategically:

- Use language that focuses on outcomes and results.
- Be more entrepreneurial.
- Think and act as a consultant.
- Focus on performance.

USE LANGUAGE THAT FOCUSES ON OUTCOMES AND RESULTS

Chapter 1 mentioned that one of the roles the trainer plays is that of message carrier. Whenever something new is introduced in the organization, the training department often is called upon to help spread the word. This can take place as part of a training program, workshop, or as a group or one-on-one session with employees. Trainers are also called upon to consult with managers and leaders of various business units to advise them on what actions to take to deal with issues involving increasing productivity and improving employee performance. How the trainer handles situations such as these has a great deal to do with whether he or she is perceived as credible and ultimately whether both the trainer and the organization come out winners.

What does this have to do with language? Perhaps more than you think. The language or words that trainers use often makes the difference in whether they are able to use their power to influence the direction their organization should be taking. In fact, trainers, like those in other fields and industries, have their own vernacular to describe what they do and how they do it. Trainers have become accustomed to using language that can be best described as soft. In fact, other than those dealing in the technical arena, trainers are often associated with helping people develop "soft" skills, and so it seems to make sense that trainers would use soft language. Depending on the situation, trainers often use such terms as facilitating, brainstorming ideas, using a nominal group technique, conducting role plays, using triads or dyads, and speaking with subject matter experts (SMEs).

Of course, there is nothing inherently wrong with using this kind of language. Problems can arise, though, when trainers use these words—called process words—with their customers to depict the services they can provide for them. A process word describes an approach, what the trainer will do or use to accomplish the training goals. Make no mistake, customers are interested to some extent in the approach that the trainer will use to accomplish the training goals. Customers, though, are mainly interested in the results that they can expect from investing their time, energy, and money in the training. The strategic trainer is always focused on, and speaks in language that emphasizes, results first and process second.

What does this language sound like? It is language that paints a picture in the mind of the customer about what he or she can expect as a result of participating in the training intervention, preferably expressed in quantifiable, measurable, or, at the very least, in qualitative terms. It emphasizes performance improvement and increased productivity, not just changes in thinking and behavior. When speaking with a customer about expected results, the strategic trainer uses action words, such as achieve, conduct, make, produce, and perform, and is less apt to use words, such as understand, identify, and list. Even before the trainer puts pencil to paper and develops objectives for the training, he or she is setting the stage for the customer in terms of expectations.

These expectations often include a clear delineation of roles to ensure that the training is successful and that anticipated results are achieved. The strategic trainer uses words that truly express the trainer-customer relationship as a partnership. It can be something as subtle as replacing phrases such as "what *I* will do and achieve" with "what *we* will do and achieve." This language includes the customer in the entire training process, because the customer is the one with the most to gain or lose. Perhaps the words that most separate the strategic trainer from more traditional trainers are: "Is this training going to make a difference in helping our organization (or business unit) achieve its goals and accomplish its mission?" With shrinking budgets and competition on every corner, a trainer's credibility is on the line unless he or she can ensure that the organization's investment in training is worth the effort of everyone involved.

BE MORE ENTREPRENEURIAL

These days the word *entrepreneur* is applied to every business in the profit and not-for-profit sectors. It used to be that an entrepreneur was the person down the block who ran the grocery store or the retired businessman who opened up the ice cream shop in the mall. Now the word *entrepreneur* has taken on an expanded meaning and no longer refers only to being the sole proprietor of a business. To be an entrepreneur in your organization requires you to think like an entrepreneur. Entrepreneurs think of themselves as the captain of their enterprise, the person who ultimately is responsible and accountable for its success. For trainers to think like entrepreneurs means they must view themselves as owners of their training enterprise and not just as caretakers. This concept runs counter to much of the thinking that goes on in training today. Traditionally trainers have been more likely to react to situations presented to them than to search out opportunities for their services to be used in ways to help their organizations achieve success. Unfortunately, when trainers do this they give up their power to influence their organization in ways that will help it achieve its mission and goals. When trainers relinquish their power, their credibility becomes vulnerable.

To get a better feel for being an entrepreneur in your organization, think about someone whom you would consider a successful entrepreneur. Next, ask yourself what makes him or her successful. Chances are that you consider him or her intelligent or knowledgeable, but these traits, though certainly important, appear somewhere down the list of reasons for their success. High on your list were probably less tangible characteristics: his or her ability to know and anticipate what customers want, delivering it with speed and accuracy, constantly finding innovative ways to deliver products and services, or maybe creating overall value for customers. These traits encourage the customers to return time after time. Successful entrepreneurs understand that they will enjoy prosperity only if their customers prosper too, so they make it a habit to listen to them and treat all their stakeholders with dignity and respect.

What can you do to think and act more entrepreneurial? Here are 10 easy-to-implement actions that you can take:

- *Create your own training mission statement.* Create a document that says exactly what the training function or department is in the business of doing and the standards it will live by. Publicize the mission statement throughout the organization. When a request comes to you for training, only do what fits with your mission. This will help you stay focused on your strategy for helping the organization achieve its mission and goals. You will become more credible in the eyes of your customers when you follow through on what you say you stand for.

- *Think and act in terms of the bottom line.* Think about how important it is to talk results with customers. For many customers this means bottom-line results. If your organization is in business to make a profit, make training part of the equation. For example, help customers make the connection between training and increasing profits, sales, and productivity, as well as its effect on decreasing big money expenditures, such as turnover, lost customer counts, and product waste. Stay away from training activities that are "nice to do," but have little effect on helping the organization grow.

- *Build a network of resources and learning.* Do not think that you have to know all the answers. Build a network of resources, including people, books, videos, and training tools. Be a resource that people come to for answers. If you are unable to meet a customer's needs, know where to find people both inside and outside of your organization who can help, and know where to locate the right tools. When you build a network of resources and learning, you expand the options available to help your customers. This, in turn, helps them feel more confident that you will be able to help them satisfy their particular needs, all of which makes you appear more credible in their eyes.

- *Have the courage to say no.* Do not make the mistake of always assuming that the customer is right. If a customer asks for something you cannot deliver or if what the customer needs is, in your estimation, not a training intervention but something else, have the courage to say so. As a trainer, you have a responsibility to help your customers make the right decisions. If what you are being asked to do is outside your mission and purview or if it does not help the organization or business unit achieve its goals, then you must raise these issues with your customer and, if appropriate, your immediate supervisor as well. Too many trainers have lost credibility by remaining silent and placing themselves and their customers in the untenable position where both parties end up losing.

- *Network, network, network.* The power of networking has taken on almost mythic proportions. Most of what you read and hear about it, however, has to do with networking with people outside your organization. Just as important, as a way of acting entrepreneurial, is to build and nurture your internal network. Get yourself known inside your organization by asking to be invited to business unit meetings, attending organization-wide functions, and spending a part of every day with customers and potential customers. Your success, in many ways, depends on the relationships you develop with key people in your organization. Remember that it is difficult to have credibility with people who do not know you.

- *Market yourself and your services.* It was once thought that all marketing activities resided in the marketing department. This was especially true of trainers who for years operated under the belief that if you build a training program, they will come. Because people today have time in their schedules for high-priority items only, trainers need to market their services in a way that not only informs people about what services are available but also creates value for their customers and encourages them to participate. Examples of good marketing tools include publishing a training newsletter to update employees on various training activities, using the organization intranet system to publicize events, and writing a column for an organization-wide publication. These items not only allow you to inform employees about training activities, but they also provide you the opportunity to increase your credibility with your customers by demonstrating your knowledge of various subjects or explaining your stand on issues important to your organization.

- *Check out the competition.* Be involved in helping your organization differentiate itself from its competitors by expanding your focus. Most trainers spend their time only looking inward. There is danger in this insular approach. To better support their organization and help it achieve its mission and goals, entrepreneurs look to the outside at what their competitors are doing to be successful. Create your own intelligence reports and inform those who need to know about your findings and then work with them and others to use training as a way of gaining a competitive advantage. Trainers who take the initiative to search out new opportunities to provide services to their organization are usually afforded more credibility, because they are viewed as active participants in the process of helping the business grow and not just someone standing on the sidelines.

- *Look for sponsors.* Like an entrepreneur who looks to people who are in the business of supplying capital to help their organization grow, consider who in your organization can provide capital in the form of support or sponsorship to help ensure the growth of the training enterprise. These are the people whose support stamps a label of unquestioned approval and credibility on your mission within the organization. Look for people in your organization who meet this criterion and have shown their support for training in the past. Solicit their input and ask for their backing in helping training achieve its mission. This can come in many forms: kicking off the first day of a training workshop, lending their name to a letter announcing an upcoming program, or handing out certificates at the conclusion of a training program. Keep the sponsors involved and share any success you receive with them.

- *Visit a valued customer.* Ask a valued customer to give you feedback on how well you are providing service, and ask how you can improve in the future. Take this feedback and relay any pertinent information to others who have a stake in this customer's success. Discuss what changes, if any, need to be made to better serve this customer in the future, and then make an action plan to implement the changes. Next visit someone who is not your customer, but who should be, and find out what you need to do to make him or her become your customer in the future.

- *Always say thank you.* As every good entrepreneur knows, the best business is repeat business. Entrepreneurs who make an effort to follow up with their customers to monitor results and ensure satisfaction are the ones with thriving businesses. The other thing they do is say thank you for letting me serve you. You will be amazed at the reaction you receive. Most people in business are not used to hearing these words, especially when delivered by someone who has just provided a service to them. Try extending this practice to others in the organization who were involved in producing or implementing the training activity. Remember to thank the audiovisual technician, the people in the printing department, and those in food service who supplied your coffee and Danish pastries, and especially your sponsors. If you really want to solidify relationships send a note or email to everyone who participated in your training activity, thanking them for attending. It is important to remember that as a trainer your very existence depends on satisfying and keeping your customers. Think of ways to make your customers feel special, and you will help ensure that they will remain your customers in the future.

THINK AND ACT AS A CONSULTANT

A theme that you will see throughout this book has to do with the changing role of the trainer. This change has not only evolved, but it has also come out of necessity. In the same way that the American public has increasingly demanded higher quality, more variety, and reasonable prices in the services and products it buys, so too has the business world. Certainly, expectations are higher now for the delivery of training services. As more organizations begin to take a critical look at the service provided by trainers and the cost involved, questions continue to arise about the return on often-sizable investments.

Thinking and acting as a consultant can make a difference. Consultants, by their very nature, act strategically in much of what they do. After diagnosing the problem, they must come up with a plan or strategy to deal with it. Sometimes they implement the plan, follow up, and measure the results. Consultants are rarely afforded the time to just try things here and there until something works. When you think and act as a consultant, your approach to your work as a trainer changes. The consultant does not always have the answers and may not even be an expert on an issue he or she is working on. Rather, the successful consultant is one who knows what questions to ask, knows how to probe to get at the underlying reasons for the problem, and then makes appropriate recommendations for its resolution. They ask such questions as: "What do you see as the problem?" "What do you see as possible causes of the problem?" "What are you or others doing that may be contributing to the problem?" "What improvements would you like to see?"

Certainly, a consultant does more than ask questions. Consultants, however, exemplify the attitude and approach that trainers need to take to help their customers achieve their goals. This change toward thinking and acting as a consultant does two things. First, it changes the customer-trainer relationship from one in which the trainer takes the primary responsibility for the success of the training intervention, to one in which both parties are involved as partners to achieve the training goals. Many trainers can point to times when they allowed themselves to be placed in a situation where responsibility for "fixing" a problem was put squarely on their shoulders, as their customer remained uninvolved only to return later, expressing disappointment in the results of the training. Experienced trainers know that only with the cooperation and involvement of their customers can they both expect to achieve success.

Second, in a purely practical way, thinking and acting as a consultant means being more focused on your customers and their specific needs rather than trying to force their needs into whatever program or workshop you have available. You need to concentrate on gathering as much information and data necessary to make a sound diagnosis of the problem(s), so that you can make an appropriate recommendation to resolve it. From a strategic standpoint, serving in the role of consultant helps you to guide your customer to make sound business decisions that not only take into consideration the unit's individual needs but also the needs of the organization as a whole. It is important to remember that customers are more likely to give credibility to people they believe will serve their best interests and with whom they have a relationship.

FOCUS ON PERFORMANCE

Perhaps as much as any change in recent years, the emphasis on human performance improvement (HPI) has transformed training from a purely tactical practice to a strategic one. People who focus on performance are often called performance consultants. Robinson and Robinson (1995) describe the performance consultant as "someone [who] thinks in terms of what people must *do* if business goals are to be achieved. This is different from the traditional training process of focusing on what people need to learn."

For many trainers the leap to HPI and being a performance consultant is a substantial one, especially for those working in organizations not quick to change. The goal of this book is not to suggest that you suddenly stop being a trainer and start being a performance consultant. Frankly, there is room for both disciplines. Rather, the goal is to have you look at your role as trainer and help you decide where to expend your time and energy to establish your credibility and help your organization be successful. When you make HPI your goal, you are acting strategically. As Fuller and Farrington (1999) point out, "Performance improvement is focused on improving the organization's ability to achieve its objectives. It looks at outcomes that are valued by the organization, typically measured in cost, quality, quantity, or timeliness."

The more you focus on performance, the more you begin to see that training is not the answer to every issue presented to you. This change in thinking automatically expands your role in helping your organization and its employees be more successful and makes it possible for you to use your power of influence in ways well beyond the classroom. Of course, with anything new, there is always some resistance. Organizations have traditionally viewed the training function only in terms of programs and workshops where people are sent to learn. With performance consulting, though, the action is closer to home as the focus becomes how employees are able to perform their work. For some, this change means that there is more at stake when performance issues are identified. As those who favor performance consulting over training point out, the transition to this new way of serving their organization is a gradual process. Chapter 10 offers an in-depth look at ways of incorporating a performance perspective into your work as a trainer.

BECOMING A STRATEGIC TRAINER

Perhaps you have already mastered some principles of strategic thinking, but other areas need some work. Using self-assessment 2-1, find ways to utilize the four actions that help trainers act and perform more strategically.

In chapter 3, you will see how understanding your organization's business affects your credibility and power to influence its success.

Self-Assessment 2-1.
Acting more strategically in your organization.

Use language that focuses on outcomes and results.

1. Look at the last training proposal or correspondence you wrote to influence someone in your organization to take an action. Did the language reflect more process or more outcomes and results? If the language was more process-oriented, jot down some ideas here for changing the way you write to reflect results and outcomes for future reference:

☐ Writing style change: _____
☐ Writing style change: _____
☐ Writing style change: _____

2. Create a mission statement that reflects what you want the training enterprise to stand for. Share it with colleagues and especially with your customers and incorporate their feedback into the document as you see appropriate. Write it here:

☐ Training mission statement:

Be more entrepreneurial.

3. Make a visit to some of your organization's competitors to see what they are doing to create value for their customers. If this is not possible, visit some local businesses that are comparable in some way to yours and take note of how they operate. Bring this "intelligence" back to your organization and use what makes sense in improving your service to your customers. List some of your observations here:

☐ Observation: _____
☐ Observation: _____
☐ Observation: _____

4. Begin scheduling visits to your valued and your soon-to-be-valued customers, and use the feedback as part of your strategy to provide the best service possible to all your customers in the future. List a few of your valued and soon-to-be-valued customers, and identify some possible discussion points here:

☐ Discussion point: _____
☐ Discussion point: _____
☐ Discussion point: _____

continued on page 20

Self-Assessment 2-1.
Acting more strategically in your organization (continued).

Think as a consultant.

5. On a scale of 1 to 10, with 10 being the highest, rate your skill as a consultant serving your organization.

    1   2   3   4   5   6   7   8   9   10

6. If you scored yourself 7 or below, think about what you can do to be more consultative in your approach when working with your customers. What immediate actions can you take to begin this process?

    ☐ Action: _____
    ☐ Action: _____
    ☐ Action: _____

Focus on performance.

7. What three actions can you take immediately to focus attention on human performance improvement in your organization as a way of helping it achieve its strategic goals?

    ☐ Action: _____
    ☐ Action: _____
    ☐ Action: _____

3

Knowing Your Business

"To most people, which is to say 99 percent of those who don't sport the letters 'CPA' or 'MBA' after their name, financial statements—the fundamental data that show how a company is doing—might as well be written in Sanskrit" (Case, 1995).

 BE A PART OF HELPING YOUR BUSINESS ACHIEVE ITS STRATEGIC GOALS.

One thing can destroy your credibility as a trainer more quickly than anything else: a lack of understanding of the business your business is in. Knowledge really is power in today's business world. For a trainer, this means that the more you know, the more you are able to use your power to influence. Take, for example, the large accounting firm that hired a training specialist to design and facilitate management training programs for its partners and staff. The trainer was very technically competent, having worked for a number of years in the pharmaceutical industry, but lacked any substantial experience in the accounting field. As is often the case, the trainer's new firm wanted its time management program up and running quickly and to be ready for deployment throughout the country in about two months. The trainer felt comfortable designing and developing the program based on previous experience. Yet, in the trainer's haste to complete the development phase of the project, she did not take time to go into the field and see what the accounting business was really all about. More important, the trainer did not visit accounting staff members for a first-hand look at the time management issues they were facing, nor did she try to establish an initial relationship with the target audience. Instead, the trainer relied on co-workers in the corporate office, including many nonpracticing accountants, who provided their own perspectives on the accounting business and the target audience.

The result was a disaster! Despite the program's wealth of valuable information and excellent facilitation by the instructor, the participants in nearly every class were quick to recognize the trainer's lack of working knowledge of their business.

The audience was particularly struck by the trainer's lack of understanding concerning the challenges they faced daily in the field. They badgered the trainer with questions, using language only someone with their experience could understand. The trainer's credibility was destroyed at the outset of program. This lack of credibility not only cost the firm thousands of dollars, but the program was eventually scrapped. A year later the trainer was forced to leave the firm.

CREDIBILITY IS ALWAYS AN ISSUE

This scenario could have been prevented if the organization had recognized that the trainer's credibility would be an issue in this situation. The trainer's manager could have suggested that she spend some time in the field as a way of learning about the business and to get a feel for the target audience. At the very least, the company would have been wise to pair the new trainer with an experienced, "credible" trainer to conduct the training. Although the organization could have done much to prevent this fiasco, the responsibility to take the appropriate steps to guarantee the success of the program was really on the trainer. The trainer could have suggested, during the design phase of the program, that some time in the field with the target audience would be a good idea. The trainer might have even used these experiences in the actual training. Instead of relying on "corporate" accountants, who had a somewhat biased opinion of what was happening in the firm, to help develop the program, the trainer could have arranged to meet with staff members who were actually working in the field. As this scenario proves, training conducted by someone without credibility is usually doomed to failure.

Of course, hindsight is always 20/20. It is easy to think of instances when a trainer has gotten into trouble not because of a lack of training skill but because of a perception that he or she was "not one of us." It is easy to fall into this trap and doubly hard to get out. In their desire to serve their organization and move quickly, some trainers rely too heavily on their training skill to get by and pay too little attention to the more subtle aspects of their work, such as whether they will be perceived as credible by their audiences. Trainers who are perceived as not understanding the business of their company or organization are simply not credible or, as one vice president put it, act like "corporate weenies who breeze in and breeze out."

It is important that you understand how your customers perceive you. You cannot rely exclusively on the comments they write on an after-class evaluation form. You need to know how they evaluate you on credibility issues, such as your overall company knowledge, industry knowledge, and general awareness of how the company measures success and makes a profit. As in the case of the trainer in the accounting firm, these issues are magnified when a trainer comes into a situation with little or no experience in the business or industry in which he or she will be working. This can even be a problem for someone who becomes a trainer after having worked on the operations side of the business. Sometimes these individuals face more subtle resistance as their former colleagues view them as suddenly out of touch with what is happening in the business today.

ESTABLISH A PERSONAL CREDIBILITY REPORT CARD

How many times have you evaluated yourself on credibility issues? For example, when was the last time you read your company's annual report? When did you last read a book not on a training-related subject but on a topic having to do with your company's industry? Do you know if your company or organization is on track to meet its sales and profit projections for the year? If you cannot answer all these questions, you probably need to do more to learn about your organization's business and industry.

You need to establish your own credibility report card as a way of keeping informed about what is happening in the business and industry you are providing services for. Your credibility report card can help you monitor your customers and their perceptions about exactly what they expect you to know. The reason is simple: Without their support, you will have little success. You have probably heard the statement: "You don't understand; our business is different." This belief exists in practically every business and industry and suggests that somehow each one is dramatically different from the other. Although as a trainer, you may recognize the greater truth that each business is different but not unique, your customers' perception is the frame of reference by which they will judge your credibility. In many ways, demonstrating your knowledge of the business is more important to your customers than demonstrating your knowledge about effective training.

WHAT CUSTOMERS REALLY WANT

When a customer drives three hours and takes time away from his or her normal work duties and family to sit in a classroom for two days, that customer wants and expects that you as a trainer are believable and trustworthy. Customers want someone who can relate on a level that suggests an awareness of their experience, who understands their work environment, and who has the skill to help them improve their performance, both professionally and personally, to achieve success on the job. To have the confidence to follow, customers must believe that the trainer understands and represents the direction of the organization. As much as they expect the trainer to know their business, they, too, want someone who can help them better understand how what they do affects the growth and prosperity of the business. Of course, customers want a competent trainer—someone who has the ability to help them learn and develop both personally and professionally. What customers really want, though, is someone who is credible enough to be considered one of them.

What can a trainer do to better understand the business his or her company or organization is in and be perceived as credible? Here are some easy-to-implement actions you can take:

- Live in the field.
- Become more financially literate.
- Take a course or develop a course.
- Go on sales calls.
- Learn about the industry your business is in.

LIVE IN THE FIELD

Of all the actions you can take to get to know your business, nothing compares to getting out and "living" in the field amongst your customers. Credible trainers make a point of spending some time each month being with their customers. Doing this may seem obvious, but in reality it happens much less frequently than it should. Too often trainers are caught up in the business of simply developing and conducting training programs and lose sight of their mission to serve the organization and its people. You cannot learn about your business, your customers, and the needs of both by staying in the cocoon of the training department, isolated from the action happening where your customers live and work.

When you visit your customers, two things happen. First, and foremost, you see your business as it really is, and you experience the issues that confront the managers and employees day in and day out. Whether your business provides services or products, is for-profit or nonprofit, visiting the field gives you the opportunity to, at the very least, become aware of the processes involved in arriving at the outcomes your business generates. A trainer must be familiar enough with the business to be able to help their customers link what happens in the training classroom to what happens in the real world, and understand how this all affects the organization achieving its mission and goals. Although the trainer should not be expected to know every detail of every job, he or she should be familiar enough to understand the goals of each function, department, or job and how they relate to the overall organization achieving its goals. For example, the trainer working with food service workers in a hospital does not have to know how to prepare the meal but should know what happens to the meal once it is prepared and how the right meal gets to the patient's room. Only with this understanding and frame of reference can a trainer expect to win the confidence of the customer and be perceived as credible.

Second, when you live in the field for a time, your relationships with your customers—the people who determine your success—begin to change. Because trainers are accustomed to seeing their customers in a classroom setting, one that is generally more comfortable for the trainer than for the customer, going to the place where the customer lives alters this dynamic significantly. The power to influence, which comes quite naturally as a result of your being in charge standing in front of the classroom, is now shared with your customers, allowing them to influence your thinking by helping you better understand their business. The experience of leaving your comfort zone and entering your customer's milieu helps break down any barriers that may exist between your role as a trainer and the people you serve in the field. As a result, the more you demonstrate a willingness to reach out and learn from your customers, the more knowledge you will gain about the business and the more credible you will appear in their eyes.

BECOME MORE FINANCIALLY LITERATE

A second action you can take is to work at being more financially literate. Traditionally, the trainer's role has been geared toward helping to train managers to manage people. Trainers trained employees to be more effective on the job but did not always help them to make the connection between what they did and how the company as a whole profited. Consequently, financial issues, such as profit and bottom-line results, have not always been a driving force behind what trainers do. Until recently, being financially literate was rarely considered a competency or requirement for the job. In fact, for some trainers, the idea of mixing training with making money was almost anathema, because the goal of creating profit seemed at odds with helping people grow and develop.

Of course, anyone working in a business today, even in a nonprofit organization, knows that this thinking is no longer acceptable or realistic. To be credible now, trainers must be able to link training to their organization's bottom-line results and show how training helps employees achieve the organization's mission and goals. This means that trainers must develop a whole new way of thinking and commit themselves to learning as much as they can about their business, especially as it pertains to its finances and achieving its strategic goals. Consider this question: "How can you expect to be credible and support the development of managers and even employees, who are asked every day to make critical financial decisions, if you do not understand how to link the training you are providing to those decisions?" The answer is you cannot. The people you train do not operate in a vacuum and neither can you.

So, what can you do? A good starting point is to make an appointment to meet with your organization's chief financial officer or the person in your organization responsible for managing its finances. Naturally, if protocol dictates checking with your immediate supervisor before taking this action, do this first. When you and the chief financial officer get together, open the conversation by explaining your purpose for the meeting: to gain a greater understanding of the financial side of the business so that you can ensure that whatever training you provide is aligned with meeting the organization's strategic goals. Then, you may continue by asking five very basic questions:

1. What are our organization's strategic goals? (You may be aware of these, but it is often helpful to review them with someone who comes from a financial perspective.)
2. What can the training enterprise do more effectively to help our organization achieve its strategic goals?
3. What measures are in place to determine whether our organization's goals have been achieved?
4. How is the organization's budget developed? (If you are not involved in developing the training budget, your next question should be: How can I ensure that I am part of this process for the next budget development?)
5. How do I read our organization's profit and loss statement? What do I really need to understand from it to meet more effectively the training needs of our organization?

Whether you need to ask all of these questions or just some of them depends upon how much information you need for you to do your job more effectively. As you speak with your organization's chief financial officer, you will probably think of additional questions to ask. The most important thing is how you act on what you learn. Your goal should always be to provide the most relevant training possible to your customers—training that helps them contribute to achieving organizational and personal goals. Most of your customers have individual goals that should be tied to organizational goals. When you provide training that helps them achieve their goals, your customers can perceive the value you bring to the organization more clearly and begin to see you as a credible contributor to their and the organization's success.

TAKE A COURSE OR DEVELOP A COURSE

A third way to gain a better understanding of the business and acquire greater financial literacy is to do something that you have probably suggested others do in other circumstances, that is, attend a course or program that teaches the basics of business finance. For example, the American Management Association and other reputable organizations offer some excellent finance for nonfinancial managers programs. As the title suggests, these courses are specifically designed for managers (and future managers) who could benefit from more exposure to the language and fundamental principles of finance to do their job more effectively. One trainer in a large international corporation who went to one of these programs came back so enthusiastic that he decided that every support staff and front-line manager could benefit from such a course. Instead of asking the organization to send them all away for a program at what would have been a prohibitive cost, he decided to develop an in-house program to give managers a good basis for making the many financial decisions they were forced to make each day. The program was an instant hit, because many of the managers discovered ways to improve their bottom-line results, thereby improving the organization's performance and helping the managers achieve the financial goals that translated into bonus money for them. Needless to say, after the success of this program, the trainer's credibility rose considerably as his customers began to view him as someone who not only understood their business, but, even more important, understood them and their needs.

Of course, the idea of helping employees understand exactly how their contribution affects the success of their organization is nothing new. For example, Freiberg and Freiberg (1996) describe how at Southwest Airlines every employee is made aware of the number of customers needed in order for the company to make a profit. This information helps employees connect what they do with satisfying their customers and ultimately helping the company to achieve its financial goals. For Southwest Airlines, the key is not just simply supplying knowledge to employees. It is helping employees use this knowledge in such a way that everyone—the organization, employees, and customers—wins. Case (1995) takes this approach even further by encouraging organizations to literally open their books to employees so that they understand exactly how the business makes money and what their role is in helping it do so. According to Case, the more employees know, the more productive they will be, and the more successful the organization will be in achieving its goals. When you take this kind of strategic approach—connecting training to helping your organization achieve its mission and goals—it is easy to see how powerful your role is in helping shape the direction of your organization and also how critical it is for you to keep your credibility intact.

GO ON SALES CALLS

If you ask veteran trainers where in their organization they seek information about their business or industry that no one else seems to know, inevitably they point to the sales department. The reason for this is simple: Salespeople not only know your organization's products and services, they understand the wants and needs of the people who matter most—your organization's customers.

One way to take advantage of this excellent resource is to ask to go on sales calls with a member of your organization's sales staff. Choose someone who has been around the business for a while and who has demonstrated a successful track record. Use this time to ask specific questions about your organization's products and services. What improvements have been made recently? Which ones will be phased out in the future? What will be added in the future? The reason for asking this type of question is simple; what you know about your products and services often helps drive your training efforts. When you understand your organization's products and services, as well as what your organization's customers are purchasing, you begin to get an excellent view of your organization's future that will help you determine where to expend your training efforts.

On a sales call, you get to see and listen to customers, the end users of your organization's product or service. Knowing customers helps provide you with a perspective of your business that is different from what you are probably used to. For a trainer this information can be a valuable way to relate training to your business's future needs. For example, on one such visit to an existing client in a re-bid situation, a trainer learned that what separated his company from its competitors was good customer service. As long as high-quality service continued, the company would maintain the business. After discussing this with the salesperson, he discovered that customer service seemed to be the prime issue for a majority of her customers. When the trainer returned to his office, he shared this information with his manager and others in the organization. Consequently, they decided to resurrect a customer service training program that had been successful a couple of years ago. With a few tweaks, the program was rolled out again and prove to be just what was needed to help retain present clients and create new sales.

LEARN ABOUT THE INDUSTRY

Another reason to look to your sales staff as a resource is to learn more about the industry your business is in. Often salespeople's perspective of the industry is the most up-to-date because they need to stay on top of current industry trends and constantly monitor their organization's competitors. This kind of information helps give you an edge when discussing training plans with those on the operations side of the business. Strategic trainers have credibility because they know where their industry is headed and gear their training efforts in that direction and not necessarily where the industry stands today. By using this knowledge, you are in a much better position to make the kind of training decisions that will help your organization grow and prosper in the future.

Is this all you need to do to know about your business? No, but these suggestions offer an excellent place to start. Even if you believe that you know your business, it is important to remember how often things change. It does not matter whether you are providing technical training or soft-skill training, your ability to provide the kind of training service that will make a difference in your organization's success depends to a great extent on your understanding of all aspects of your organization's business and industry. Make an effort to find people in your organization who have knowledge that can be helpful to you, and try to "pick their brains." Read as much as you can about your business and industry, so that you become fluent in the language. A good rule of thumb is that you should work just as hard to establish credibility by knowing your organization's business and industry as you work to establish your credibility by knowing the training field.

THE CHOICE IS YOURS

If you and your colleagues cannot help your organization achieve its goals, then your organization probably will not survive. Or, if it does, it may do so without you. This may sound harsh, but it is the reality today. The choice is yours: Either understand your business and how you can contribute to its success, or you risk being perceived as lacking credibility and no longer needed by the organization. That is the *real* bottom line. To get an idea of the work you need to do to know your organization's business, take self-assessment 3-1.

In chapter 4, you will learn how to interpret your organization's culture as a means for identifying and implementing the most relevant training and development opportunities for all employees.

Self-Assessment 3-1.
Actions you can take to better know your business.

1. On a scale of 1 to 10, with 10 being the highest, rate how well you know the business your business is in.

    1   2   3   4   5   6   7   8   9   10

2. Now, rate how well you know the industry your business is in.

    1   2   3   4   5   6   7   8   9   10

If you scored yourself 7 or below, begin to think about what you need to do to better get to know your business and/or industry. What immediate actions can you take to begin this process?

☐ Action: _____

☐ Action: _____

☐ Action: _____

3. Design your own business knowledge credibility report card. For example, try grading yourself on the following issues, using a scale of A (excellent) through F (failure). Then add one or two of your own issues and grade yourself. Finally, give yourself an overall grade and list some actions you can take to improve your "grades."

☐ I am familiar with what is contained in my company's latest annual report. Grade___

☐ I read books on my company's industry-related subject. Grade___

☐ I am knowledgeable about my company's sales goals and make an effort to track our performance. Grade___

☐ I know my company's strategic goals and make an effort to track our performance. Grade___

☐ My own issue: _____ Grade___

☐ My own issue: _____ Grade___

What final grade would you give yourself? ___

What immediate actions can you take to improve your grades?

☐ Action: _____

☐ Action: _____

☐ Action: _____

4. Make arrangements to visit some field locations or, if you work in a one-location facility, some different departments where your customers and potential customers are. Make a list of items you would like to learn from them.

☐ Item 1: _____

☐ Item 2: _____

☐ Item 3: _____

continued on page 30

Self-Assessment 3-1.
Actions you can take to better know your business (continued).

5. Make arrangements to meet with your organization's chief financial officer to learn more about your organization's finances. Develop a list of ideas about how you can better contribute to helping your organization achieve bottom-line results.

☐ Idea 1: _____

☐ Idea 2: _____

☐ Idea 3: _____

6. Research a business finance course that you may want to take and decide whether any meets your particular needs.

7. Discuss with key people in your organization whether they perceive the need and value of offering a business finance course in-house.

8. Make arrangements to go on a sales call. If this is not possible or practical, arrange to meet with member(s) of your sales staff to learn as much about the business and industry as you can from them.

4

Understanding Your Organization's Culture

"'Values' is such an overused term that I wouldn't bring it up if it weren't really important. But if I am going to talk about the difference between winners and losers, I have to talk about values. Just about every big organization in the world has a formal ethics or values statement hanging on the wall somewhere. So it's not saying anything special to note that winning companies have them as well. But unlike run-of-the-mill companies and outright losers, winners actually pay attention to their values. They think about them *and* they live them" (Tichy, 1997).

 KNOW YOUR ORGANIZATION BOTH INSIDE AND OUT.

If you want to get a good introduction to what organizational culture is all about try visiting a Ritz-Carlton hotel. Of course, if you can stay for the night, all the better, but at least allow yourself the pleasure of walking around and observing how those who work at the hotel conduct themselves. Notice how they address the hotel's guests, each other, and most especially how they treat you. Take some time to watch the hotel's guests and observe their expressions. Listen to the conversations between guests and hotel workers in the lobby and on the floors of the hotel. Look around at the physical layout of the hotel, the pictures on the walls, and the signage giving directions. Finally, ask someone behind the desk or at the bell stand a question, perhaps where to find the restroom or where to get a cab, and see how he or she responds.

For those who have had the opportunity to spend any time at a Ritz-Carlton hotel either as a guest or, as in this case, a curious observer, you know exactly what this exercise is meant to show. Such a strong culture exists at the Ritz-Carlton organization that even someone from the outside can sense it just by spending a half-hour walking around. The Ritz-Carlton's motto is "We are ladies and gentlemen serving ladies and gentlemen." This statement, perhaps more than at any other organization, truly exemplifies what the Ritz-Carlton stands for. In fact, if you go to any of the 35 hotels worldwide or encounter some of the 15,000-plus employees who work for Ritz-Carlton, you will be treated with a consistency that mirrors the corporate motto. The reason for this is very simple: The culture at the Ritz-Carlton accepts nothing less.

What does this have to do with your credibility as a trainer? Every organization has a culture—a set of beliefs, values, and standards that set the tone for how employees are to act, how work is to be done, and what image is to be portrayed to the world. Some organizational cultures, such as that of Ritz-Carlton, are very strong, whereas others are less well defined. Nevertheless, every organization's culture has the power to help determine whether an organization will be successful or not. As a trainer, you must be able to understand and work within your organization's culture, especially as it relates to the training and development of employees, so that you can be credible and successful. Not every organization has a culture as well defined as the Ritz-Carlton's, making it all the more important for you to learn how to interpret your organization's culture, so that you can effectively support the training and development of employees and help the organization achieve its mission and goals.

ELEMENTS OF CULTURE

Before you can begin to figure out your organization's culture it is helpful to understand what a business culture is all about. Deal and Kennedy (1982), in their seminal book on corporate culture, introduce five basic elements that are essential to an organization's culture:
- business environment
- values
- heroes
- rites and rituals
- cultural network.

Business Environment
According to Deal and Kennedy (1982), the business environment has the greatest effect on an organization's culture: ". . . the environment in which a company operates determines what it must do to be a success." Different cultures seem to fit different kinds of businesses. For example, high-technology, start-up companies tend to operate in environments that are very fast-paced and informal. Decisions are made at breakneck speed. Colleges and universities, on the other hand, tend to be slower-paced, formal or informal (depending on the school's history), and are notorious for making decisions slowly.

Values
Today perhaps the most popular notion of culture has to do with an organization's values. These are the core beliefs that, according to Deal and Kennedy, define the organization's set of acceptable standards. The values, often expressed in stories and lore, embody for the organization's employees what they need to do to be successful. The values also help guide decision making at every level of the business,

within the framework of the organizational strategy. Some organizations live their values and demonstrate these beliefs every step of the way. Freiberg and Freiberg (1996) point to at least 13 core values at Southwest Airlines, including "profitability, family, fun, individuality, and legendary service," which help sustain the organization and make it one of the world's most successful airlines.

Heroes

Deal and Kennedy (1982) define the organization's heroes as those individuals who "personify the culture's values and as such provide tangible role models for employees to follow." Interestingly, not all heroes occupy or have occupied a seat in the executive suite, nor are they necessarily still alive today. In fact, some have been ordinary workers who happened to have had an extraordinary effect on their organization. It is not unusual, for example, to hear about the 35-year volunteer whose "heroic" service inspired the local hospital to name a wing after her and whose picture at its entrance serves as a legacy to the committed service she provided.

Rites and Rituals

As you may guess, the rites and rituals that are part of an organization's culture serve as the frame of reference for employees about what behaviors are acceptable in the course of their day-to-day activities. These rites and rituals can include many things, from the systems, procedures, policies, and politics of the business to "casual Fridays" to the yearly extravaganza that one large financial services organization puts on every year, complete with a six-course dinner and celebrity entertainment. These activities have significance in that they provide a strong message to both employees and outsiders as to exactly what the company stands for and what it expects from them.

Cultural Network

According to Deal and Kennedy (1982), the cultural network serves "as the primary (but informal) means of communication within an organization." This network provides the means for sending the values and corporate folklore throughout the organization and is an essential way for employees to understand exactly what is happening around them. It pays to know who the key players are in the network because they are usually the people who know exactly what is going on. When you ask them for the "skinny," you often get an insider's look at how the organization truly functions. Some people who seem to naturally be a part of this network are top executive administrative assistants, office receptionists, and, of course, the telephone operators who seem to be clued in to just about everything happening at their companies.

CERTAIN THINGS "DON'T FLY"

Unless you understand the basic elements of your organization's culture, you may have problems influencing its future. Even veteran trainers have been stopped in their tracks while attempting to develop or implement a program because their organizations' cultures would not allow or support it. The reason for this is that in every organization certain things "just don't fly." This can be especially frustrating to trainers when they know that their organizations can truly benefit from instituting a particular training initiative they have in mind.

The fact is you need to be aware of the cultural components of your organization and be sensitive to how they play out. For some, especially those trainers who have been a part of their organization for a while, the organization's culture is less a mystery and something merely to be maneuvered through. Even for these people, though, it is often worthwhile to revisit basic assumptions they have made about their company, especially after the arrival of new leadership or a drastic change in the business or industry. Two situations that have almost become common and can certainly affect an organization's culture are the merger of two organizations or a corporate downsizing. In these two instances especially, it is extremely important to recognize that what once was will not necessarily be in the future. For some organizations in the throes of massive change, established beliefs, values, rites, and rituals may be pushed aside as new ones begin to emerge.

NEW PRACTITIONERS ESTABLISHING CREDIBILITY

For new practitioners and those who are attempting to establish credibility in a new organization or position, it is even more important that they quickly become familiar with their organization's culture. Credibility is, at least in part, about acceptance. Many well-intentioned, but inexperienced, trainers have come into an organization and, believing changes were necessary, attempted to introduce new ideas and ways of thinking and doing business only to find an entrenched culture that is resistant to change. To deal effectively with this resistance, it is important that you first seek to learn about and understand your organization and its culture before taking any action, because there is a very good chance that you may not have a second opportunity to do so.

It is not unusual for trainers to find themselves in a position where they are being asked to help "change" their organization's culture. For the trainer who is eager to respond to the needs of their organization, this type of request can lead to a "culture abyss," from which the trainer never emerges. To think that training alone can change a culture is to think that someone can take a class in conversational French, go to Paris, and talk like a native Parisian. It clearly does not work that way. As one veteran trainer said, "If I could do that, I'd be worth millions and retired."

INTERPRET YOUR ORGANIZATION'S CULTURAL READINESS FOR TRAINING

Trainers need to understand the power of an organization's culture, and, in so doing, be respectful of it. Of particular importance to trainers is their organization's readiness to incorporate training as an integral and influential part of the business. One way to do this is to learn how to interpret your organization's cultural readiness for training so that you can strategically use your power to influence your organization in a credible way. The more you understand how your organization works, the easier it will be to establish your credibility, contribute to your organization's success, and achieve your own success.

Trying to interpret your organization's readiness for training can be quite a challenge. This is especially true because some of the elements of the culture may be very clearly presented, and others may be less so. Several other variables—for example, your experience with your organization and any major changes that have occurred—may also complicate the picture. You can see that the process may take some time. As a trainer, however, it is important to understand your organization's culture so that you can use your power to influence in a positive way and make good training-related decisions. You must remember that your credibility is tied directly to how well you are able to recognize and work within some of the subtle and not-so-subtle aspects of your organization. To help you begin interpreting your organization's culture and its readiness for training, try taking self-assessment 4-1, using Deal and Kennedy's five elements of culture as a guideline. If you are new to your organization, you will need to do a bit more sleuthing and some questioning of those you believe are in a position to know about your organization's culture. As you answer the questions, write down your responses so you can check them later.

YOU CANNOT CHANGE THE CULTURE OVERNIGHT

Although you cannot change your organization's culture overnight, you can begin to affect the perception your organization has of the value of training. In so doing, you become a credible participant in your organization's success. To change any negative perceptions requires a change in thinking. First, start by reassessing the role of the training enterprise, as well as your role, in helping your organization achieve its goals. Next, ask yourself if the training enterprise operates in a way that is in alignment with your organization's culture, its values, and the way it conducts business. If you find that it is not, this may be limiting you in terms of using your power to influence your organization's success. For example, you may work in an organization that values the development of all its employees, but if your training function only provides developmental opportunities for supervisors and mid-level managers, you may be out of step with what is truly important in helping your organization be successful. These lost opportunities can spell disaster for your credibility.

Finally, review the questions in self-assessment 4-1, paying close attention to those that you answered negatively. Consider the issues central to being consistent with the business environment:

- living the organization's values
- relating to key people, role models, and heroes
- maintaining compatibility with rites and rituals
- accessing the cultural network.

Using self-assessment 4-2, identify the areas that require your concentrated effort. Focus on these areas to help establish the training enterprise, yourself included, as a viable and relevant component in your organization's success.

In chapter 5, you will learn the importance of marketing yourself and your services, and you will discover the most effective steps you can take to be successful.

Self-Assessment 4-1.
Questions to ask about your organization's culture.

Business Environment

1. Would you characterize your organization as progressive and one where   Yes/No
   individual and organization development and learning are considered
   very important?

2. Is your industry dependent on training and development to be successful?   Yes/No

3. With regard to training, does your organization keep pace with its competitors?   Yes/No
   For example, some industries, such as banking, tend to be more training-
   intensive than others.

4. When senior managers talk about the future, a major change initiative, or a   Yes/No
   new line of products and services, do they usually make sure a representative
   from the training enterprise is present?

5. Is your organization known in the industry for a particular strength or   Yes/No
   competency and does training play an integral part in supporting it? For
   example, companies that are sales-driven often have an extensive sales
   training curriculum.

6. Is training routinely mentioned in internal publications, such as newsletters   Yes/No
   and updates, or in external correspondence, such as the management
   discussion portion of the company's annual report, press releases, sales
   proposals, marketing materials, brochures, and Websites?

Values

7. Is there a statement that describes the organization's core values?   Yes/No

8. Are these values clearly presented in ways so that employees, customers,   Yes/No
   vendors, and so forth will know them?

9. Do all employees know what the values are?   Yes/No

10. Does your organization support employee training and development with   Yes/No
    adequate funding, staffing, and commitment from senior management?

11. As part of its recruiting effort to perspective employees, does your   Yes/No
    organization advertise employee training and development as a company
    value?

12. Does your organization use training and development as a primary resource   Yes/No
    to help employees improve performance, as well as achieve and maintain
    company standards for success?

13. Are individual development plans constructed for all employees?   Yes/No

14. Does your organization reward people for developmental achievements?   Yes/No

15. Is it rare that a slated training program is cancelled or that individuals   Yes/No
    scheduled to attend upcoming sessions are pulled out of the sessions?

Self-Assessment 4-1.
Questions to ask about your organization's culture (continued).

Heroes

16. Is there a tradition of demonstrated support for the training enterprise by respected present and past company leaders? — Yes/No

17. Are there individuals, past or present, with direct or indirect connections to the training enterprise who are considered to be company heroes? — Yes/No

18. Is there at least one credible leader in the organization who serves in the role of sponsor and whose support almost always guarantees training success? — Yes/No

19. Is there a senior leader whom you can count on to kickoff and conclude most training sessions, lending a degree of importance and credibility to every training event? — Yes/No

20. Are there heroes in the organization, past or present, who have set the tone for learning and development in the organization? — Yes/No

Rites and Rituals

21. Does your organization consider employee training and development an integral part of how it conducts business? — Yes/No

22. Is the rollout of new training interventions done with some fanfare? Are they routinely kicked off by a senior-level company official and concluded with the issuing of certificates by the same official or another organizational leader? — Yes/No

23. Is there a clearly delineated set of standards for design, location, quality, organizational commitment, evaluation measures, and so forth by which all training interventions are carried out? — Yes/No

24. Is the commitment of employees and managers to training and development so strong that there are built-in consequences (penalty fees, for example) for missing or canceling out of a program? — Yes/No

25. Are training and development opportunities available and encouraged for employees at every level of the organization, including front-line employees, supervisors, middle managers, senior managers, and executives? — Yes/No

Cultural Network

26. Is employee training and development routinely celebrated through mentions in organization-wide or public correspondence and publications (e.g., company newsletters, marketing tools, sales proposals)? — Yes/No

27. Does the network for announcing new training programs and initiatives extend beyond mailings? For example, are there regional or business-unit HR or training representatives responsible for publicizing training news and events? Is there an intranet system that provides up-to-date training information? — Yes/No

28. Is participation in training and development programs and initiatives as active away from the "corporate" office as it is where the corporate leaders reside? — Yes/No

continued on page 38

Self-Assessment 4-1.
Questions to ask about your organization's culture (continued).

29. Do credible individuals, who are supporters of training and part of the cultural network, frequently use the network to sing the praises of the training enterprise?   Yes/No

30. Are there stories that have been passed down that paint particular training and development programs or initiatives in a very favorable light?   Yes/No

What the Answers Indicate

Add up the number of times you responded "yes" to the questions. For many trainers, answering these questions is a real eye-opener and may explain some of the difficulties many trainers have exerting their power to influence. If you answered yes to at least 15 of these questions, the chances are that you are working in a culture that views training and development as a positive force in helping the organization grow and achieve its goals. The potential for you to establish credibility in this kind of environment is better than most.

For those who answered yes to fewer than 15 questions (probably the majority of trainers), your task is a little more difficult. Your organization's culture may not be quite ready for the training enterprise to be a strategic partner in helping your organization grow and achieve its goals. Although this makes it a little more difficult for you to gain the credibility you need to make a difference, it also presents opportunities to introduce the kind of changes necessary for your organization to achieve success.

Self-Assessment 4-2.
Actions you can take to better understand your organization's culture.

1. On a scale of 1 to 10, with 10 being the highest, rate how well you understand your organization's culture.

    1   2   3   4   5   6   7   8   9   10

2. If you scored yourself 7 or below, begin to think about what you need to do to better understand your organization's culture. What immediate actions can you take to begin this process?

☐ Action: _____
☐ Action: _____
☐ Action: _____

3. Conduct your own mini-audit of your organization's culture, paying special attention to Deal and Kennedy's (1982) five basic elements of organizational culture:

☐ Business Environment: _____
☐ Values: _____
☐ Heroes: _____
☐ Rites and Rituals: _____
☐ Cultural Network: _____

4. Of the areas you see as weaknesses, decide which ones you want to devote your attention to. What immediate actions can you take to begin this process?

☐ Action: _____
☐ Action: _____
☐ Action: _____

5. Assess your role and the role of the training enterprise in helping your organization achieve its goals. What immediate actions can you take to strengthen each one of these roles?

☐ Action: _____
☐ Action: _____
☐ Action: _____

6. Determine if these roles are consistent with your organization's culture. What immediate actions can you take to help make it more consistent?

☐ Action: _____
☐ Action: _____
☐ Action: _____

7. Ask others whom you respect—both inside and outside your organization—about their perceptions of your organization's culture. Ask for their feedback regarding their perceptions of its readiness for training. What actions, if any, can you take based on this information?

☐ Action: _____
☐ Action: _____
☐ Action: _____

5

Marketing Yourself and Your Services

"The relationship between a seller and a buyer seldom ends when the sale is made. In a great and increasing proportion of transactions, the relationship actually intensifies subsequent to the sale. This becomes the critical factor in the buyer's choice of the seller next time around" (Levitt, 1986).

 SUCCESSFUL TRAINERS ALWAYS MARKET THEMSELVES AND THEIR SERVICES.

It does not matter how good you are if no one really knows about it. These words are especially true for many in the training profession, because trainers, in general, are not natural marketers of themselves or their services. The belief that "if you build it (a program, that is) they will come" has persisted since the days when trainers developed as many programs as they could, issued them as part of a training curriculum, and then sat back, waiting for people to sign up. Though still happening in some companies today, this approach no longer works because the result is often a hodgepodge of courses with minimal appeal to perspective customers, little connection to the organization's goals, and weak backing and commitment from the organization's leadership.

THE FIRST RULE OF MARKETING FOR A TRAINER

What is required today is something different. To establish credibility, trainers must take it upon themselves to think in terms of marketing, selling, and promoting themselves and their services each day. This mindset is important because it puts the responsibility to do this squarely where it belongs—on the shoulders of the trainer. Some may find the process of marketing themselves and their services distasteful or uncomfortable and against what they stand for as a trainer. If this is your feeling, your idea of marketing may be somewhat dated or clouded by the image of a slick marketer packaging some snake oil remedy for management's problems and trying to foist it on the unsuspecting. This conception could not be further from the truth, because the first rule of marketing for a trainer is to remember that what you are marketing is something of value for your customers. Think of it in these simple terms: The marketing component of your job is all about creating a perception in your customers' minds that they are deciding to use a valued service that will help them fulfill their wants and needs.

UNCOVER YOUR FEELINGS ABOUT MARKETING

There are many ways to market yourself and your services; some of the most important ones are covered in this chapter. To develop a marketing strategy, start by taking an introspective look at yourself. This process helps you to establish what value means in your own mind first. To do this, try taking self-assessment 5-1 to get a better understanding of how you feel about marketing yourself, as well as the products and services you offer. See how many statements you can respond to affirmatively.

To successfully market yourself and your services, you need to be able to respond affirmatively to each statement in the self-assessment. If you cannot, perhaps it is time for you to rethink your role as a trainer in your organization. You must have a mindset that says, "I believe in what I am doing, I think that what I do adds a great deal of value to the success of my organization, and I want to share it with others."

CREATE A MARKETING STRATEGY

Now, assuming that your responses in the self-assessment were all affirmative, then you need to focus your attention on creating a strategy that meets the following three criteria:
- The strategy conforms to both the training enterprise and organization mission and goals.
- The strategy is consistent with the amount of resources you have available to deliver what you promise.
- The strategy includes effective ways of getting you and your message out to your customers.

To build your strategy, you must think like a business, understand your customers' needs, and educate your customers. The following sections focus on these three elements of a successful strategy.

Think Like a Business
The first part of your strategy should start with the way you think. When most people think about marketing, they think in terms of business. This means that you need to think in terms of the training enterprise within your organization as *your* business; you have a very important stake in its success. The fact is businesses only stay in business if they have customers—satisfied customers. Because this is your business, you must be the one to make decisions that will satisfy not only your customers' wants, but, more important, their needs. You can include many things in your strategy to help your business grow and help you be perceived as credible by your customers and the many individuals in your organization who have a stake in your success.

Self-Assessment 5-1.
Know the value of yourself and your services.

On a scale of 1 to 10, with 10 being the highest, indicate the extent of your agreement with the following statements:

1. I take pride in my talents and capabilities as a trainer and believe that the products and services that I have to offer add value to helping my customers and my organization achieve their goals.

Disagree				Somewhat agree				Strongly agree	
1	2	3	4	5	6	7	8	9	10

2. I believe that part of my responsibility as a trainer is to inform and educate my customers about all the products and services that I can provide, as well as the benefits they will derive from them.

Disagree				Somewhat agree				Strongly agree	
1	2	3	4	5	6	7	8	9	10

3. I am more interested in establishing long-term relationships with my customers based on trust, credibility, and respect than with simply meeting today's need.

Disagree				Somewhat agree				Strongly agree	
1	2	3	4	5	6	7	8	9	10

4. I am always trying to come up with as many new and different ways as possible to let people in my organization know about what I am doing and the products and services I can provide for them.

Disagree				Somewhat agree				Strongly agree	
1	2	3	4	5	6	7	8	9	10

5. I believe that my success as a trainer depends, to a great extent, on how well I am able to instill in the minds of my customers the value of all the products and services that I can provide for them.

Disagree				Somewhat agree				Strongly agree	
1	2	3	4	5	6	7	8	9	10

Understand Your Customers' Needs

The importance of understanding your customers' needs seems like an obvious place to start, but, despite their best efforts, many trainers stumble on this step. They work diligently to try to learn about their customers' needs. Some go to great lengths to assess training needs using different kinds of instruments and tools that ask customers to respond to questions about what they believe their needs are. Unfortunately, sometimes they end up with information that is not exactly what they were looking for. For example, consider a young training manager at a growing software consulting firm. She sent out a needs assessment survey she put together by herself to all 250 employees. The manager was very pleased with the response to the survey and shared the results with the principal of the firm to whom she reported. When they reviewed the results, however, the training manager was dismayed to see that the majority of identified "needs" actually fell under the category of "nice to have," having little to do with meeting the organization's goals.

When they reviewed the survey, they realized that the questions on it were geared more toward the kinds of programs employees *wanted* and not so much about what employees *needed* to help the organization grow and be successful. Because they did not trust the data generated by the survey, the manager and principal decided to follow up with focus groups designed to uncover more specific needs of the employees. This time, the results proved more revealing. For example, rather than the stress management program asked for in the first assessment, what the employees really needed were changes in some of the work processes they used to do their jobs. Some of the processes were hindering their performance and causing them stress. Consequently, the training manager and the principal agreed that the manager would concentrate her efforts on dealing with the cause of the stress, in this case improving the work processes, rather than on training programs that focused on symptoms only.

What these two learned was that had they not questioned the initial survey results, they might have spent a lot of time developing and marketing programs that, even when implemented, would have done little to address their customers' real needs. Even worse, what they produced would have made no significant difference to the success of their organization. No amount of advertising, promotion, brochures, or publicity can make up for not recognizing what your customers' needs are. It is easy for trainers to fall into this trap when they spend thousands of dollars and hours and hours of time designing and producing glitzy marketing materials to promote their training curricula. What they really need to do is devote more time and money to ensuring that their customers have a product or service that is designed to truly meet their needs. Fail to do this and you will have a disappointed group of customers and lose your credibility as a trainer.

To find out what your customers' needs are, you need to use your creativity and make a concerted effort. You can use formal needs assessment tools, focus groups, surveys, brainstorming, nominal group techniques, or any number of other tools and instruments. Remember that a successful business is one that is always asking its customers what they want and need; do not just assume that the answer they gave last week is the same as today. You do not need to wait until you are ready to do a formal needs assessment. When you run into people whose opinions you respect and who are representative of your customers, ask them questions, such as "What would make performing your job easier?" or "If you could choose one skill to improve the way you perform your job, what would it be?" or "What is the biggest obstacle that stands in the way of meeting your customer's expectations?" The idea here is not that you will be able to meet every need brought to you, although certainly by asking the question you do, in effect, raise expectations. Your credibility comes with the exchange of ideas that takes place. It comes also with how you treat these requests and the honesty and commitment you show your customers in help-ing them understand not only what their present situation is, but, more important, what the future can be.

Educate Your Customers

It is interesting to note that although trainers are in a business closely linked to the field of education, they do not always take the time to educate their customers or do not do a very good job of it. How many times have you heard trainers say, or maybe said yourself, something like: "They say they want training, but they don't really know what they want!" The usual reaction trainers have to this kind of situation is to become frustrated with their customers and wonder why the customers cannot say what it is they need. As frustrating as this situation is, it does present a real opportunity for trainers to educate their customers to better understand their needs and can help trainers determine appropriate courses of action to satisfy those needs. When you serve your customers in this manner and help them to see possibilities where before there was only confusion, you become more credible in their eyes. For example, many of your customers may see you only as someone who conducts train-ing programs. By educating your customers, you are better able to expand their awareness of other kinds of training interventions, which may be more appropriate for their particular situations. Many times these interventions, often focusing on improving specific performance deficiencies, are smaller in nature, more cost effec-tive to implement, and have enduring effects.

Credible trainers, like good business people, understand the value of educated customers and take every opportunity to ensure that they are aware of all the kinds of services the trainer can provide. Trainers who take the time to educate their cus-tomers usually find it a worthwhile investment and are rewarded in ways that cer-tainly make up for any time spent doing so. For example, educated customers, because they are more knowledgeable about what to expect and the benefits they will obtain, are often more committed to ensuring the success of the training ini-tiative. This commitment often translates into less time wasted for the trainer and increases the chances for both parties to succeed. In terms of marketing, of course, the educated customer is also one who will look for opportunities in the future to use your services, helping to strengthen the importance and credibility of your training business.

How can you help educate your customers? You can try some of these actions:

- Ensure that your customers have the most up-to-date information on your products and services.
- Invite potential customers to visit while you are conducting a program or are involved in work on a training project so that they can see firsthand the kinds of services you can provide for them.
- Conduct one-hour mini-workshops over lunch on hot topics of interest to your customers and the organization.
- Send a copy of an article or book on a hot topic to key individuals in your organization along with a note explaining why you think they may benefit from reading the particular selection. Then, follow up and ask them for reactions to what you sent.

- Send along notices you receive regarding outside training programs and workshops to individuals in your organization who may benefit from such programs, and create a training bulletin board to inform all employees about outside learning opportunities.
- Keep a database of articles, books, videos, and computer-based training materials on various training- and business-related topics that you have in your library and send out the listing to all managers for distribution in their departments.
- Convene a training council of individuals who value training; the council charter should provide for educating and informing employees about training issues and organization-wide learning opportunities.
- Invite outside presenters to speak to employees at departmental, regional, or companywide meetings on issues important to your customers and the organization.

Another great way to educate your customers is to publish a training newsletter. A newsletter is an excellent marketing tool for helping your customers and, just as important, lets potential customers know what you are doing and what is happening in the training arena. For some, the idea of publishing a training newsletter sounds like a daunting task, involving monthly or bimonthly publication of a document consisting of multiple pages. More doable, though, depending on the amount of support available, is a newsletter containing one double-sided page that comes out either two, three or four times a year. Newsletters normally consist of schedules of events, articles on training-related topics, the names of recent program graduates, and a message from the training director or other company leader. Whatever you include, just remember that this is a marketing tool designed to grab attention and educate your customers so that they will decide to use your services. It is not supposed to provide everything they need to know about training and development. So keep it simple and to the point, bearing in mind your customers' needs as the basis for what you print.

A newsletter provides you with an excellent forum for using your power to influence and share your thoughts and ideas about the direction your organization is headed and the role you and the training enterprise play in helping it get there. Doing this is a tremendous credibility builder, because your customers naturally want to know what you believe in and what you stand for. A newsletter keeps you and the training enterprise in front of your customers and potential customers. Even if they do not read anything you write or only glance at it for a few seconds before throwing it away, your customers and potential customers over time will learn about what you do and, when they are ready, know where to go to get help.

If you decide to publish a newsletter, it is important to remember that whatever you produce represents you and all other trainers in your organization. This means it should look polished and professional and be well written. It should also work well within your organization's culture. For example, one young trainer found that the managing partner of the large, prestigious law firm he worked at considered the cartoon on the front page of the training newsletter to be inappropriate and not very funny. Before you embark on a newsletter, find out as best you can what your customers would like to read about in the newsletter. It is also helpful to take advantage of any resources available within your organization to write, edit, print, and distribute the newsletter. This helps keep costs down and often allows you the opportunity to leverage your relationships with people in the printing department, mailroom, and other support services to ensure that things are done right. Have fun creating your newsletter and do not be afraid to talk about what you and the others in the training department are doing. Look at this as another opportunity to demonstrate your competence and build credibility.

Another way to educate your customers is to accept speaking engagements outside of work. Some trainers take advantage of every opportunity to make presentations to groups on a wide range of topics. Although this is certainly a good way to develop professionally, it is also an excellent marketing tool for building credibility. When you do outside speaking engagements, you are demonstrating your talents and capabilities to a wider audience. These engagements can be used to publicize your capabilities within the organization.

Speaking engagements can be on an assortment of subjects and use different media. One senior training professional in a large, multidivision company, for example, heard of a Sunday morning radio show dedicated to the field of work-life balance, a subject that she had an interest in and some expertise. She contacted the station and offered to do an interview with the host. A month later, she appeared on the half-hour show. Although the program was on at seven in the morning and did not have a large audience, several people in her organization, many of whom did not know her, heard her on the show. As word got around her organization, the HR director at a large division called her and asked that she give a presentation on balancing work and family responsibilities. She had never worked for that division before, but the presentation eventually led to a number of additional assignments in the division working on some HPI projects. All of this came about because of the radio appearance. The lesson: Sometimes the best marketing occurs when you least expect it.

TRAIN OTHERS TO MARKET

Sometimes trainers view the marketing of training services from a rather narrow perspective. Too often, trainers think that the only individuals in a position to market training are trainers themselves. This is not so! Although trainers are normally in the best position to market training services, other individuals play an indirect but important role in marketing these services. They are the people who make up the different links in the value chain of the service you provide: the people who print your materials, who work in the facilities where programs are conducted, who provide the Danish pastries and coffee at breaks and lunchtime meals, and who set up the rooms for you to conduct training sessions. These people all affect in some way how successful you are in meeting the needs of your customers.

How many times have you spent months determining your customer's needs, and then developing and conducting a great training module, only to receive evaluations afterward that talk only about the problems with the room temperature and poor quality of food that was served? This, unfortunately, is the perception these people carry away, and no amount of marketing in the future will change the way they feel about you and the service you provided. The fact is the people who provide support for you also represent you and what you are trying to accomplish. They, too, must understand what you are trying to achieve and the standards you require in the service you and they are providing. In many ways, they are marketing you and your training services for the future, and you need to pay attention to how they present themselves and their service because your credibility depends on them.

Here is a simple way to help do this: The next time you are conducting a program, write down the names of all the individuals who are part of your value chain, the people who help you provide value to your customers. Next, determine what they need to know in terms of your standards, expectations, and objectives and write it down. Last, schedule a time to sit down and review these things with the individuals who are key to your success. You may ask, is this marketing? The answer is yes. The perception that people have of you and your service extends well beyond the quality of the materials you supply and how well you make a presentation before your audience. It is also about their perception of how others represent you and the training enterprise. When you pay attention to the little things, not only do you help guarantee the quality of the training you are involved with presently, but you also help ensure that people return in the future. These are the things that will help keep your credibility intact.

GET TESTIMONIALS

People who own their own businesses have known for years that one of the best ways to attract new customers is to have them speak first with satisfied customers. They know that without new customers the chance of staying in business will diminish quickly. Successful trainers understand this, too. Yet, when was the last time you asked a satisfied customer for a testimonial or an endorsement about the work you performed for them? If you answered never or rarely, you are in the majority. This is why it is so critical for you to think like a businessperson. Asking for testimonials and endorsements comes pretty naturally for business people who are marketing their services. This step needs to become a part of the way you conduct your business too.

For example, if you develop and implement a successful behavioral-interviewing training module for your organization's mid-Atlantic region, why not ask the regional vice president if she would be willing to speak with her counterpart in the southeast region who may be contemplating doing the same thing? You can take this further, by asking the mid-Atlantic vice president to participate in an interview for the training newsletter about the behavioral-interviewing training and how it benefited the region's recruiting and retention efforts. It is important to recognize that this is a business—your business—and businesses are successful only if they keep their present customers satisfied and attract new ones. It is all right to toot your own horn now and then, as well as have others do it for you. The credible trainer provides a service that has value and enjoys informing people about it. Do not be afraid to ask for help from your satisfied customers to spread the word about the value that your service has for your organization. Remember that it is their business too.

Another group to get involved in helping you market your services are your sponsors. Ask them to endorse the work you and your colleagues are doing.

Because your sponsors are often organization leaders, their endorsements usually carry a great deal of weight. Your sponsors are also probably politically savvy about the way your organization works. This can be helpful as you maneuver through your organization's culture, getting the word out about what you can do and the services you can provide. Perhaps more than anything else, though, your sponsors are often in the best position to vouch for your credibility, so ask for their support and take advantage of any offer they make to help you carry out your marketing strategy.

UNDER-PROMISE AND OVER-DELIVER

You have probably noticed a recurring theme in this book, and that is the perception that training's traditional role is changing. Nowhere is this trend more evident than in the greater emphasis on HPI, the current push for trainers to focus on services that help achieve organizational goals, and the growing popularity of new methodologies, such as action learning, which provide people with the opportunities to learn by doing. Keeping up with these changes requires different approaches and modalities than have been used in the past. There is a very good chance, though, that you may not yet be prepared for or be sufficiently comfortable with providing these kinds of services to your customers. You are certainly not alone. Of course, as you learn more about these new ways to meet your customers' needs you will gain more competence and confidence in using them.

As you broaden your role as a trainer and begin to incorporate new approaches and technologies into your range of services for your customers, bear in mind this caveat: You must be able to deliver what you promise. There is an old saying that goes, "Under-promise and over-deliver." This is sound advice as you decide what services to market and the strategies you will use for marketing them. If your resources are limited, either use your power to influence to obtain more or accept that you will not be able to provide all the services you would like. Consider also that in your role as a consultant, you have the ability to save your customers much time and money by helping them understand that training, specifically in the form of programs and workshops, may not be the answer to every problem they have. Nevertheless, you must be in a position to provide, or arrange for other experts to provide, the kind of service that will make the most sense for each customer. Use self-assessment 5-2 as a guide for developing a marketing strategy. As you consider your marketing strategy, a good rule of thumb to follow is to market only that which you can effectively deliver, because your credibility and the fate of your customers is on the line.

Chapter 6 explores another role that a trainer can play: champion of learning.

Self-Assessment 5-2.
Develop a strategy to market yourself and your services.

1. On a scale of 1 to 10, with 10 being the highest, rate how well you market yourself and your training services in your organization.

    Need
    improvement   Average   Effective
                                                                              marketer
       1   2   3   4   5   6   7   8   9   10

2. If you scored 7 or below, think about what you can do to do a better job of marketing to your customers. What immediate actions can you take to begin this process?
    - ☐ Action: _____
    - ☐ Action: _____
    - ☐ Action: _____

3. Review your responses for self-assessment 5-1. If you answered no to any of the questions, think about what is preventing you from answering affirmatively. What immediate actions can you take to turn a negative response to a positive?
    - ☐ Action: _____
    - ☐ Action: _____
    - ☐ Action: _____

4. What are your main strategies for marketing yourself and your services to your customers?
    - ☐ Strategy: _____
    - ☐ Strategy: _____
    - ☐ Strategy: _____

5. Which one of your marketing strategies works best? Why?
    - ☐ Best Strategy: _____
    - ☐ Why?: _____

6. What marketing strategy would you like to start using or use more often? What immediate actions can you take to begin doing these things?
    - ☐ Strategy: _____
    - ☐ Action: _____
    - ☐ Action: _____

7. Ask your sponsors, leaders, and trusted colleagues what they think about your marketing efforts. Given their responses, what immediate actions can you take to improve your efforts?
    - ☐ Action: _____
    - ☐ Action: _____
    - ☐ Action: _____

Self-Assessment 5-2.
Develop a strategy to market yourself and your services (continued).

8. What resources need to improve or increase that will allow you to do the kind of marketing in your organization that will make a difference in achieving its goals?

☐ Resource: _____

☐ Resource: _____

☐ Resource: _____

9. What immediate actions can you take to improve or increase resources available for marketing yourself and your services?

☐ Action: _____

☐ Action: _____

☐ Action: _____

6

Being a Champion of Learning

"Because so much of our conscious experience with learning is in activity that someone else has assigned to us—a parent, a teacher, an employer, someone we're competing against—learning for many of us is a *means to an end that is not of our choosing.* We go through a learning process in pursuit of a goal we have been told is important. As beginners, we are goaded with reasons for beginning, and those reasons are the learning goals that have been given to us" (Vaill, 1996).

 COMMIT TO CONTINUAL EMPLOYEE LEARNING AND DEVELOPMENT.

Not long ago, the subject of learning, which heretofore received only lip service in many organizations, took on new importance when the term *learning organization* was introduced into the American business lexicon. Senge describes a learning organization as one "that is constantly expanding its capacity to create its future." In such organizations, all employees are encouraged and supported to make lifelong learning an integral part of their development. As many businesses have discovered, however, creating and sustaining a learning organization has been a task much easier said than done. In fact, outside of a few, highly publicized organizations—General Electric, Motorola, and the Harley-Davidson Motor Company, to name three—that live up to the basic tenets of a learning organization, it is the rare organization that is truly committed to continual employee learning and development.

This is not to suggest, though, that the ideals of the learning organization are without merit and not worth pursuing. In fact, nothing could be further from the truth. All you need to do is look at the success of General Electric, for example, to recognize that something very special is going on in organizations dedicated to employee learning and development. For a company to become a learning organization requires more than simply labeling itself one. What it takes is a strong commitment and effort and, as in the case of Jack Welch at General Electric, someone to serve as the driving force to make continual employee learning and development a valued and integral part of how the organization does business and achieves its goals.

CAUGHT UP IN THE HYPE

Many organizations, anxious to jump on the bandwagon, have been quick to get caught up in the hype surrounding the notion of becoming a learning organization, some falling victim to a "by-the-numbers" approach to achieving their goal. This usually happens after some senior executive reads the latest business book or attends a seminar, then sends out an announcement declaring his or her company a "learning organization," and assigns someone, often a trainer or other HR professional, the role of making it happen. Of course this does not work because a company cannot become a learning organization or even establish learning as a company value by edict. What many fail to understand is that learning is not a commodity to be departmentalized and assigned to someone, only to be rolled out and put on display when it is convenient to let everyone know how important it is.

What is clear is that there is no simple formula, no step-by-step process to make a company a learning organization. Like most new business concepts, a major problem with becoming a learning organization is trying to figure out exactly what one is. The nature of the subject is such that there is often a clash of interpretations as to what kind of learning truly makes a difference from a business perspective. In the end, though, whether your business considers itself a learning organization or even wishes to become one is less important to its overall success than what it holds to be true. Organizations committed to continual employee learning and development seem to all hold the following three ideals:

- The organization holds true the ideal that continual learning and development of all employees is something that adds value to the way it conducts business.
- The organization holds true the ideal that continual employee learning and development is an important part in how it will achieve its goals.
- The organization is ready and willing to commit the necessary resources, time, and energy to make continual employee learning and development a company value.

The next step in this process of commitment toward employee learning and development requires someone to take the lead and inspire others to follow—what it takes is someone to be the champion of learning.

A CHAMPION OF LEARNING

Perhaps of all the different roles a trainer may play in the organization, none is more challenging than that of being a champion of learning. Although it may seem a fitting role for a trainer, it is certainly not one that comes automatically. Champions are people who serve their organizations as advocates, wholeheartedly associating themselves with a cause or principle. The champion's role, as many trainers know, is not an easy one since they are constantly faced with resistance from people who may genuinely disagree with the position they represent or from those who simply are not open to change. Although champions are not necessarily expected to assume responsibility that obligates them to be answerable and accountable for the success of their beliefs, what makes their role such a challenge is that, in many companies, the line between being a champion and assuming responsibility is often fuzzy. In these situations, the champion's plight is similar to the person who, after courageously raising a thorny issue in a meeting, finds herself assigned the task of fixing it.

A champion of learning plays a critical role in helping the organization achieve success through the continual learning and development of its employees. Along with his or her other training responsibilities, a champion of learning speaks to the value of continual learning and development and establishes credibility by raising issues, generating ideas, challenging the status quo, and serving as a primary resource for all learning and development issues. In this role, they serve as both facilitators of action and catalysts for change. A champion of learning operates from the belief that although each individual must take responsibility for his or her own learning and development, the organization must assume overall responsibility for creating an environment and supplying the means for employees to exercise this responsibility. Above all, a champion of learning is resolute in his or her belief that an organization can only achieve its goals and be successful if there is a commitment to continual learning and development of all its employees.

Champions of learning constantly demonstrate their credibility by being knowledgeable both about their organization and about what employees need to learn to help it accomplish its goals. They serve as models to others by living what they espouse through their personal pursuit of their own learning and development and are skillful in the way they use their power to influence the thinking of others. Champions do this within a context that includes

- the goals their organization wishes to achieve in the future
- their organization's leadership's level of support
- their organization's cultural values
- their organization's strengths and weaknesses
- their organization's past history regarding change
- their organization's fiscal health
- the current and predicted future state of their organization's industry
- their competitors' strengths and weaknesses.

STRATEGIC BUSINESS PARTNERSHIPS

Champions of learning recognize that their ability to influence the direction of their organizations is limited. To counter these limitations, they work diligently to form and maintain close working relationships with many people throughout their organization, enlisting others who believe in the value of continual learning and development for employees to join their cause. The way they do this is to establish strategic business partnerships with key individuals in the various business units and departments in their organization. This allows the champion to spread his or her message through more "local" champions whose credibility is already established in the organization. By leveraging their relationships with their strategic business partners, a champion of learning is more likely to gain credibility through associations with these key individuals. These associations, in turn, provide the champion with greater opportunities to spread his or her influence throughout their entire organization.

THREE MAIN GOALS OF CHAMPIONS OF LEARNING

To be successful, all champions of learning must dedicate themselves to achieving the following three main goals:

- to affect the thinking and attitudes of the people in their organization toward continual employee learning and development
- to reinforce the value of continual employee learning and development as a means to achieving organizational goals
- to help lead people to take appropriate action to establish an infrastructure that will support continual employee learning and development as an organizational value.

To be an effective champion of learning and accomplish these goals takes more than simply having the ability to speak out about issues related to learning to those in your organization. To be successful, you must be able to make a convincing argument that shows how continual learning and development supports your organization's overall strategy for achieving its goals. This requires the champion to be a catalyst for action, thereby establishing a rationale that warrants his or her organization making the financial investment and cultural shift necessary for this to happen. Although there are many reasons for an organization to move in the direction of establishing employee learning and development as a company value, the five reasons explained in the following sections make a clear-cut case for doing so.

Reason 1: The Face of Business is Changing

As a champion of learning, your biggest challenge is to counter the skepticism that remains in many organizations about what is gained by investing in the learning and development of their employees. "Show me the bottom-line results" has long been the mantra of leaders who have balked at investing the dollars today to ensure their employees are equipped and trained to deal with the demands of tomorrow. Perhaps justified as a fiscally responsible stance in the short term, its long-term effect often eliminates the organization's ability to be flexible and react to change. Although some still see learning as a final destination that shares only a tenuous connection to the business itself, your role as a champion is to convert this thinking to one that views continual employee learning and development as a means, not as an end, to achieving business results in the future.

The challenge for business today is to be prepared for the changes that will come tomorrow. It once was true that in business the things worth acquiring took the form of tangible assets—equipment and property—the staples of the Industrial Age. The prevailing wisdom was whoever had the most "toys" was the winner. Today, the game is different as the Industrial Age closes, and a new age emerges. It is an age that is based on information and intelligence; the winner is not the one who has accumulated the most things, but rather the one who has gained the most knowledge and the ability to use that knowledge to make wise decisions about the future. In this age, to paraphrase Thomas Stewart (1997), "the product of knowledge is wealth."

As technology continues to expand and new markets open throughout the world, much of what was learned in the past is rapidly becoming obsolete. This is part of the changing face of business and requires organizations to rethink what their employees will need to know in the future to succeed. Others may wish to focus on the organization doing better what it currently does now, but your role is to argue for a commitment to continual employee learning and development as a strategic means for remaining competitive and meeting the demands of the future. You will need to expand the awareness of those who perceive learning as it has existed in the past, as a formal and structured activity that only takes place in a classroom, to an understanding that learning can and does occur anytime, any-place, anywhere. As a champion of learning your message is clear: Learn or go out of business.

Reason 2: Preparing Future Leaders

Champions of learning have a responsibility in their organization to ask two questions repeatedly:
1. Where will our future leaders come from?
2. How will we develop them?

Unless the answers to these two questions point to a clearly defined, specific leadership development strategy, based in part on continual learning and development, then the champion of learning knows that the organization is vulnerable to the inevitable changes in fortune that can beset even the strongest company. Although some still hold to the notion that leaders are born, successful organizations like PepsiCo and Johnson & Johnson have a leadership development strategy that does not leave the succession of leadership to chance. They provide a culture in which a seemingly endless series of learning opportunities for leaders helps maintain a well-stocked leadership pipeline.

In their organizations, champions of learning direct the attention to the best practices of benchmark companies recognized for their leadership development initiatives that are based largely on the principles of continual learning and development. From these and other successful organizations, champions identify and may even assist in the implementation of some of the most effective leadership development methods and approaches to be included in their organization's overall strategy, including the following:

- *Action learning.* This highly experiential approach to learning provides learners with opportunities to apply in the real world what they have learned in the classroom. The process usually involves conducting individual or group projects around critical business issues between sessions. Because participants are often held accountable for the solutions they develop, motivation to learn is often higher than in more formal learning settings.

- *Mentoring.* Effective mentoring programs are ones in which the learners are trained in their roles, given the freedom to perform in their roles, and allowed the time and support to make the process successful. The concept of mentoring is almost synonymous with continual learning and development, because it entails the transfer of learning from one generation of leaders to the next.

- *Leaders as teachers.* Tichy and Cohen (1998) first introduced the idea of the teaching organization, in which leaders assume responsibility for teaching others. This model is considered to be something of an alternative to the learning organization. According to Tichy and Cohen, a critical component of being a leader is sharing learning with those who are led. What often occurs in organizations where leaders are also teachers is that the entire learning process assumes a far more important status than in organizations where learning is transmitted only through trainers in a classroom.

- *Executive development programs.* Many organizations dedicated to continual learning and development take advantage of outside sources to provide developmental training for leaders and future leaders. These organizations invest thousands of dollars and provide time for their leaders to participate in programs at places like Harvard, the Wharton School, and the Center for Creative Leadership in North Carolina.

- *Job rotation.* This arrangement is a useful means to help develop leaders, because it offers them the opportunity to learn about the entire business as they perform in different positions throughout the organization. This experience provides leaders with a broadened perspective of their company and helps them develop their leadership skills with people in different lines of business.

Reason 3: Recruitment and Retention

In a business world where employee loyalty has been set on its ear, recruiting and retaining the best and brightest people have taken on proportions similar to the quest for the Holy Grail. Not only top performers, but others who are in the middle of the pack but have specialized skills, now expect to be provided with developmental opportunities that will help them stay current in their present position, learn skills to advance in new careers, and enhance their chance for promotion. With many organizations more than willing and able to make incredibly enticing offers for people they want to join them, most of these high-demand employees are fully aware that if one organization does not respond to their needs, another will.

Champions of learning take this challenge seriously and advocate that their organizations adopt a formal response to this situation. Champions understand that only an organization that supports the continual learning and development needs of its employees can hope to compete in such a market. To do this, organizations must have the will to dedicate the resources and the means for employees to learn necessary skills and obtain knowledge to grow in their present positions and explore new career opportunities. To do this, organizations can offer online training opportunities, executive development programs, and leadership development libraries. One large pharmaceutical company even established a career development center for all its employees to use.

As Bassi, Cheney, and Lewis (1998) conclude, ". . . there is mounting evidence that workers are voting with their feet by leaving. They are assuming responsibility for developing their own skills, in large part, by quitting those organizations where their prospects of development seem poor in favor of organizations with more promising career development opportunities." As organizations, especially those that are technology-intensive, jostle with one another for market share, one factor may differentiate the winners and the losers: the willingness (or lack thereof) to make a long-term commitment to their employees' development. The challenge for the champion of learning is to help ensure that the organization's commitment is that of a winner and that its actions reflect this commitment.

Reason 4: Advances in Technology

Perhaps nothing makes a more practical case for an organization to commit to continual employee learning and development than the linkage between rapid technological change and a company's ability to conduct everyday business. With an ever-expanding, globalized economy affecting even the smallest of companies, success belongs to those organizations that can keep up technologically to develop and implement the systems that help deliver their products and services with the most speed to the most markets. This requires all organizations to stay on top of advances in computing and communication systems, for example, to ensure that they can continue to compete.

A major issue for many organizations, however, is not just finding and keeping people who are on the cutting edge of the many technological advances occurring daily, but also ensuring that the average 47-year-old baby boomer is able to understand what technology can do and use it to help his or her company grow and achieve its goals. The role of the champion of learning is to promote the idea that only through a commitment to continual learning and development can the organization expect to support all its employees to meet the challenges of a business world transformed by technology.

The champion must call attention to the fact that it would be naïve to assume that the organization's entire workforce consists of Generation Xers raised on computers, e-commerce, and advanced communication systems. In fact, it is a mistake to even assume that today's technology will still exist tomorrow. The champion of learning understands that many people in critical positions have not grown up in the age of information, yet are expected to perform in ways that would suggest they did. Because these people will continue to play a major part in their organization's success, the champion's task is to draw attention to the need for the organization's continued commitment to the learning and development of both the technically gifted and the not-so-gifted to ensure the continued productivity of all.

As spending on technology continues to outpace spending on training, the resulting disparity makes the champion's challenge to the organization even more clear. The champion must call attention to the need for ensuring that all employees have the benefit of learning what they need to know to stay one step ahead of the technology curve and that their continual learning and development keep pace with the rapid technological advances occurring each day. If businesses fail to keep pace, they lose good people, leaving the organization vulnerable and unprepared to compete in the future.

Reason 5: The Link to Performance

An organization's decision to invest in employee learning and development often comes down to one thing: What will the return-on-investment (ROI) be? To relate ROI to employee learning and development means looking at whether training or developmental activities will result in improved employee performance. This relationship was clearly demonstrated in a study conducted by the American Society for Training & Development (ASTD, 1999). It showed that, for the year 1997, increases in training investments made by organizations participating in the study were linked to increases in performance as based on the following five indicators:

- profitability (if applicable)
- quality of products and service
- customer satisfaction
- employee satisfaction
- ability to retain essential employees.

What was also found was that, for those organizations that participated in a 1996 study as well as 1997, there was a strong link between the investment in training in 1996 and the performance shown in 1997. This study suggests that involvement in learning and development (in this case through training) activities has a strong relationship to individual performance and that, according to the indicators used to measure the results, help not only to improve bottom-line results but have a positive effect on issues related to both customers and employees. Although the results do not prove a cause-and-effect relationship, they do suggest that the benefits of training investments persist for some time.

In a business world that too often sees the pursuit of learning and the development of people as being too soft an endeavor to have any effect on an organization's ability to succeed, the champion of learning can use data like this as a powerful tool to help reverse this belief. The champion of learning knows that not all forays into employee learning and development, or training for that matter, improve performance or yield such positive results. The champion's message is not necessarily to draw conclusions but rather to help enlighten the unenlightened. One of the greatest services the champion of learning can provide the organization is exposing people to information that flies in the face of conventional thinking and challenging those who are still skeptical about the value of learning and development.

A champion of learning does not come equipped with credibility; he or she must earn it. To evaluate how your organization values continual employee learning and development and how effective a champion of learning you are, complete self-assessment 6-1. Know that despite your best efforts, there will always be those that doubt the message and the messenger. The champion of learning recognizes that there will always be resistance, but the champion carries on, knowing full well that to those who pursue knowledge goes the wealth.

Chapter 7 takes a closer look at the value trainers gain in developing strategic partnerships with their customers.

Self-Assessment 6-1.
Actions you can take to help ensure that your organization values continual employee learning and development.

1. On a scale of 1 to 10, with 10 being the highest, rate how strongly your organization values continual employee learning and development.

Not at all				Somewhat valued				Highly valued	
1	2	3	4	5	6	7	8	9	10

2. If you scored your organization 7 or below, begin to think about what you need to do to help make continual employee learning and development an organizational value. What immediate actions can you take to begin this process?

   ☐ Action: _____

   ☐ Action: _____

   ☐ Action: _____

3. On a scale of 1 to 10, with 10 being the highest, rate yourself as a champion of learning in your organization.

Not at all				Neutral				Strong learning advocate	
1	2	3	4	5	6	7	8	9	10

4. If you scored yourself 7 or below, begin to think about what you need to do to strengthen this role. What immediate actions can you take to begin this process?

   ☐ Action: _____

   ☐ Action: _____

   ☐ Action: _____

5. How successful have you been in establishing strategic business partnerships in your organization? What immediate actions can you take to improve these partnerships and make them more productive?

   ☐ Action: _____

   ☐ Action: _____

   ☐ Action: _____

6. What is your organization doing to respond to the following questions:

   ☐ Where will our future leaders come from? _____

   ☐ How will we develop them? _____

7. What immediate actions can you take as a champion of learning to ensure that the answers to these questions are in line with achieving your organization's goals?

   ☐ Action: _____

   ☐ Action: _____

   ☐ Action: _____

continued on page 62

Self-Assessment 6-1.
Actions you can take to help ensure that your organization values continual employee learning and development (continued).

8. What is your organization doing to recruit and retain the best and brightest employees?

9. What immediate actions, as a champion of learning, can you take to improve this process?

☐ Action: _____
☐ Action: _____
☐ Action: _____

10. What is your organization doing to ensure that all employees are able to stay ahead of the technology learning curve?

11. What immediate actions, as a champion of learning, can you take to ensure that your organization succeeds by staying ahead of the technology learning curve?

☐ Action: _____
☐ Action: _____
☐ Action: _____

12. How successful have you been in equating continual learning and development with improvement in employee performance? What immediate actions, as a champion of learning, can you take to help your organization make this connection?

☐ Action: _____
☐ Action: _____
☐ Action: _____

7

Strategic Partnering

"Effective partnerships are noncompetitive. People approach such relationships as casting bread upon the water: Each contribution causes the partnership to grow and prosper. An attitude of abundance creates a legacy of affirmation that lives on in the language customers use to describe the service provider" (Bell, 1995).

 BE A STRATEGIC PARTNER, NOT A LONE RANGER.

For those who are not old enough to remember, the Lone Ranger was a television character back in the early sixties who wore a mask and fought desperados. The whole idea of the show was the classic "good guy" versus "bad guy" conflict. This show, however, had a slight twist because the good guy, dressed in white with a black mask would (with all due respect to his trusted friend Tonto) always end up beating the bad guys by himself. In fact, not long after the show had its television run, the term Lone Ranger, meaning someone who always goes about doing things on their own, became very much a part of the American lexicon.

Many trainers have historically taken a "Lone Ranger" approach to providing their services to their customers. These trainers use their experience and expertise, similar to the real Lone Ranger whose particular skill was ridding towns of bad guys, to help resolve their customers' problems pretty much on their own. Although they attempt to find out as much as they can about their customers' issues, sometimes by asking questions or maybe even going into the field to see what is happening for themselves, this is usually where things stop in terms of any collaboration between the trainer and customer. The trainer is considered the "expert" and, as such, assumes most of the responsibility for analyzing the customer's problem, determining the right solution to deal with it, and then implementing the solution, usually in the form of a training program—all with only minimal customer involvement.

Many trainers actually relish the role of being the person who "fixes" things for those customers who are ready to hand over their problems to someone else.

Because the trainer bears most of the responsibility for the project's work, he or she also has a great deal of influence in deciding its measure of success. One problem that could arise if there is little involvement from the customer is proper follow-up. For example, if the goal of the program is to improve listening skills, often what is measured is only the quality of the program or the trainer's presentation and not whether participants indeed improved their listening abilities. Assuming the program goes well, the typical outcome of all the trainer's work is an enjoyable experience for the participants but only a minimal effect on the organization. As for the trainer's credibility, it grows or shrinks based on whether the customer is satisfied with just having a "nice" program or whether the customer truly wants improved performance. This inconsistency can sometimes put trainers in an uncomfortable position, because they are usually the ones who take the heat if the project does not meet the customer's expectations.

THE ROAD TO EXTINCTION

Although this scenario continues to be played out in organizations today, most trainers recognize that the Lone Ranger approach will eventually lead them and, perhaps, their organizations down the road to extinction. Because customers are under intense pressure to improve performance and increase productivity, many tend to be more discriminating in what they want and what they want is not a one-size-fits-all program. Knowledgeable customers these days want and expect to be involved, at least in some way, in planning and implementing the training services they will be receiving. That is why to be credible today, you must work together with your customers and not separately from them. The stakes are simply too high for one person to be entrusted with all the responsibility for making the right decisions about the choice of a particular training intervention and how training objectives should be achieved.

What is needed today is a reevaluation of the relationship between trainer and customer. In this new relationship, the roles of customer and trainer are intertwined and mutually dependent on one another's contribution to a successful outcome. This relationship requires commitment—an investment by both parties to achieve a common goal that is aligned with their organization's strategy and that is much grander than either one could hope to accomplish alone. This synergy is more than the sum of two or more people working together; it is people serving each other as strategic partners.

STRATEGIC TAKES ON MANY MEANINGS

The word *strategic* has taken on different meanings depending on the context in which it is used. For the purposes of this book, a strategic partnership is one in which individuals serve one another to implement a strategy or plan to achieve a common goal that is consistent with their organization achieving its strategic goals. Not every partnership is a strategic one, and not every relationship between a trainer and customer is a partnership. For example, many times trainers will offer sessions on different business topics and open these programs up for managers and employees in their organizations to attend. In a partnership, though, especially a strategic partnership, the emphasis is on service, because when you serve another person, you give of yourself to achieve something that has value and importance for both people. In the case of a strategic partnership, this concept goes beyond the parties involved, affecting the organization as a whole. Partnerships are about sharing this service and learning from one another, always keeping the common goal as the focus. Although partnerships are not always equal nor necessarily democratic in nature, both parties only "win" if they work together as one.

In a strategic partnership, it is important for both you and your customer to mutually establish your roles, responsibilities, and accountabilities on all projects and initiatives you work on together. Among the issues that should be addressed before beginning a project or initiative are

- questions about how decisions will be made
- who will have final authority over general aspects of the project or initiative
- involvement of key people in the organization
- how the project or initiative fits into the overall strategic goals of the organization.

Because the parties in a strategic partnership may not be equal in terms of responsibility and authority, in most instances the customer's wants and needs take precedence if no consensus is reached. Nevertheless, you should never feel compelled in any partnership to do anything that you believe to be morally wrong, inappropriate for your organization, or potentially damaging to your credibility. In such instances, you need to have the courage to respectfully, yet forcefully, disagree with your customer, ask someone of stature in the organization to mediate, or, in some extreme cases, walk away.

SIX REQUIREMENTS OF STRATEGIC PARTNERSHIPS

Working as a strategic partner with your customers presents you with a great opportunity to strengthen your credibility while helping your customers and organization achieve their goals. Although you can only be expected to accept responsibility for your own actions, to help make a successful partnership you must also act and perform in such a manner that encourages your partners to follow your lead. Partnerships only work when the people involved are selfless and willing to check their egos at the door. To be successful, all parties in the partnership must commit to putting the purpose and goals of the partnership above anything else. Six requirements for a successful strategic partnership are discussed below.

- *Mutual trust, honesty, and respect.* Strategic partnerships flourish when the parties involved demonstrate mutual respect, honesty in all interactions with one another, and respect for each other's thoughts, ideas, and beliefs. In a strategic partnership, the trainer must assume the lead in modeling the behaviors that demonstrate these values. Because it is very likely in every relationship that disagreements will arise about how to proceed, it is imperative that all parties express their wants and needs in the very beginning as the partnership is forming to prevent derailment later on. Although the goal in this kind of relationship is to achieve some measure of common ground, the true gauge of strength of any partnership is the freedom all parties have to say no.

- *Shared purpose and goals.* Every partnership should be formed with a purpose in mind, and this purpose should be defined, shared, and agreed to by all parties from the beginning. To be strategic, the partnership's purpose should extend beyond merely meeting parochial needs. Although trainers should always try to work in partnership with their customers, strategic partnerships should be reserved for relationships that will have a broader effect on the organization's ability to achieve its goals.

- *Shared accountability.* In a strategic partnership, accountability is shared; that is, each person is accountable for what he or she has agreed to but also is accountable to the other parties in the partnership to achieve their shared purpose and goals. To be successful, a trainer should again take the lead in ensuring that each party understands that the partnership is only as strong as its weakest link. Although individual accountability must be established, ultimately it is the partnership that succeeds or fails.

- *Two-way communication.* Partnerships only survive if all parties engage in two-way communication that allows all of them to share openly and freely with one another their thoughts, feelings, and ideas. Because discussions about communication often end up as laundry lists of *dos* and *don'ts*, it is the trainer who can have the greatest influence by modeling effective two-way communication for their partners instead of just talking about what to do. This includes demonstrating the importance of listening actively, giving clear written and verbal messages, providing specific instructions, and giving and receiving feedback. Effective two-way communication is especially important in strategic partnerships because of the interaction the partners often have with those outside the partnership: company managers and leaders, support staff, suppliers, and others who may be affected by, or who affect, the partnership's success.

- *Shared outcomes and results.* In a strategic partnership, it is imperative that all parties be clear about and agree to the outcomes and results that they expect and want from each project or initiative in which they are involved, as well as what they expect and want from each other. Partnerships break down when there is a lack of clarity around these issues. Some trainers find it helpful to design a contract and submit it to all the parties involved. When the language and specifics have been agreed to, the partners then sign the contract with copies given to all parties. Contracts, or anything in writing for that matter, solidify agreements and serve as a reference point when questions arise about roles, responsibilities, and the like.

- *Shared tracking, measurement, and follow-up.* Strategic partnerships focus on outcomes and results. The partners must be able to track the progress toward desired outcomes and measure and follow-up on the results, not only for each project or initiative but also for the partnership itself. Usually the trainer takes the lead for ensuring that a system for tracking, measuring, and following up is in place, but all involved parties share responsibility for all three processes. What many find is that the more specific the tracking system, the easier it is to monitor the progress of particular projects, initiatives, and the partners themselves. Along these lines, it is critical that all parties understand what will be measured and how, so that they can target their performance to achieve success of each project or initiative and the partnership itself. All parties should also agree on when and how they will follow up on the results of the project or initiative, and what their next steps will be to ensure a lasting effect of all outcomes.

WHAT IF PARTNERSHIPS ARE NOT AN OPTION?

Although establishing strategic partnerships with your customers may seem like a sensible and productive thing to do, some organizations are structured in ways that prevent these kinds of relationships from ever forming. This is especially true in organizations that are highly departmentalized and in organizations that encourage and value competition, rather than cooperation, among businesses, regions, or people. Consider the example of the large national organization that set up a competition among their six regions to help stimulate new sales activity following a particularly slow year. To help support the regions, the training department offered to conduct a "brush-up" sales training program for all people involved in the sales process in each region. To ensure that the particular needs of each region and the organization's overall needs were addressed, the trainer asked to meet with each region's sales team so that they could work in partnership to customize the program. Much to the trainer's surprise, none of the sales staff from any of the regions would agree to meet with him. The reason, he later found out, was that they viewed him as an outsider who might potentially expose their sales secrets to other regions, thus giving the "competition" an advantage in making more sales and winning the contest. After numerous efforts to allay people's fears proved unsuccessful, the trainer eventually gave up on conducting the training. Even worse for the trainer, his credibility was dealt a blow, because some regions viewed his attempt at working with the different regions as being counter to the organization's culture, which valued competition among the regions above regional cooperation as a way to spur growth.

Needless to say, the trainer learned some valuable lessons, two of which helped him the next time he was faced with a similar situation. First, he learned that to truly work in partnership with your customer means taking time to build a relationship based on mutual trust, honesty, and respect, the first requirement for a strategic partnership. The trainer in this situation was not sensitive to the fact that although he was well liked as a person, he was still considered an outsider by most of the regions. Without their trust, he lacked the credibility necessary to be perceived as impartial. Since the organization's culture supported competition over cooperation, the trainer learned that even the best training program is not enough to overcome a doubting customer. For him to succeed in helping the regions he needed to deal with their skepticism first.

The second lesson that the trainer learned was that where there is neither shared purpose nor shared goals (one of the requirements for a strategic partnership), there is nothing to hold the partnership together. Clearly the trainer's purpose was to help drive sales at a time when the organization was experiencing a flat growth rate. The regional sales teams, meanwhile, had a different purpose and that was to win the contest, even if it came at the expense of what was best for the organization as a whole. In this situation, the trainer soon discovered he was in a no-win position with little chance of helping the regions and with his future credibility at stake. At that point, the only thing he could do was raise his concerns about the situation to his customers and try to influence them to change the direction in which they were headed. If that did not work, then the trainer had to decide whether it was even appropriate for him to remain involved. In this situation, the trainer's decision was the right one: move on to some other project, one in which he could make a difference.

OTHER OPPORTUNITIES TO ESTABLISH PARTNERSHIPS

There are many opportunities for you to establish partnerships with key people, both inside and out of your organization, people whom you may not normally consider customers. Although not always strategic in nature, these business partnerships, similar to the ones that promote continual learning and development mentioned in chapter 6, have a direct affect on your perceived credibility and, ultimately, your success. The following sections offer some good examples of such relationships.

Partnerships with Support Staff

As mentioned previously in this book, numerous people, representing various departments and constituencies in your organization, can affect your success as a trainer. They usually fall into the category of support staff and work in functions such as food service, audiovisual, housekeeping, and engineering, to name a few. When you are conducting a training program or producing a meeting, for example, these individuals can have as much effect on the success of the event as you do. Every trainer has been in a situation where the training room was not set up as expected so the participants are left standing around five minutes before the start of an 8:30 program waiting for the advertised 8:00 continental breakfast to arrive. There is certainly enough blame to go around for these all-too-prevalent episodes, but common to many such snafu situations are the relationships (or lack thereof) that spawn them.

Relationships in which people depend on one another to serve their mutual interests tend to break down when the parties involved are not clear about their purpose and goals and if trust, respect, and two-way communication are lacking. When the parties see their "jobs" as independent from the others' jobs, each approaches his or her actions from the perspective of what will satisfy their individual needs, not the parties' mutual interests. When this happens, for example, the housekeeper does not think to question the trainer's request for a U-shape for 15 in a room that will only accommodate 12 comfortably. Instead, the housekeeper follows the request, resulting in a last-minute scramble to reconfigure the room because neither the trainer nor the housekeeper took the time from the beginning to ensure that their collective needs were being addressed.

When your relationship is based on a partnership, however, these problems begin to go away. When people work together and develop a relationship based on trust, honesty, respect, open communication, and shared goals, the outcomes they produce are more likely to be in line with what they are mutually seeking to achieve. Partnerships based on the six requirements mentioned in this chapter help those involved build credibility with one another by allowing each individual to be in a position to better serve the others to achieve the partnership's purpose and goals. Although these partnerships are less about strategy and more about accomplishing immediate goals, to those involved they represent the best means for doing their jobs effectively. Just as a trainer does not want to worry that the classroom will not be ready, neither does the housekeeper want to be called at the last minute to rearrange the furniture. When the trainer and housekeeper work as partners, they achieve their mutually beneficial goals together and in so doing become more credible in each other's eyes and in the eyes of the organization.

Using Outside Consultants

Dealing with outside consultants and suppliers offers another example of how working in partnership can ensure successful outcomes for all involved parties. As organizations continue to outsource training, many are looking to external consultants to support the growing need to provide more training internally. Although some excellent results can be obtained by working with consultants, the potential for problems is always there if both parties are not careful. One reason for this is that when a trainer brings in an outside consultant, the trainer then assumes a new role in addition to being a service provider to the customer. The trainer actually becomes a "customer" for the consultant. For some trainers, this reversal of roles is more difficult to execute than they might have anticipated, especially if they are not willing to give up some control to the consultant to achieve the results they are both seeking.

What helps trainers under these circumstances is to think and act as they would want their customers to—as involved partners not just passive customers. The same six requirements apply, although as the customer the trainer naturally has more responsibility for making the final decisions about the project or initiative. What many trainers find surprising when they are filling the role of the customer working with an outside consultant is that some consultants are comfortable with working in partnership, whereas others are not. Then it is helpful for the trainer to model the behaviors associated with working in partnership and educate his or her "partner" in ways of making the relationship work.

As the customer in this situation, the trainer needs to raise the issue of working together as partners even before the project or initiative begins. The consultant's views regarding working in partnership should be a factor to consider during the proposal phase of the project or initiative, when the trainer and the organization are evaluating the consultant's credibility and deciding whether to use the consultant or that particular firm. Before the decision is made, the trainer needs to express his or her expectations clearly to the consultant. The trainer must also ask the consultant to verbalize his or her own expectations about the project or initiative and solicit opinions about what the working relationship will be. Working up front to establish the partnership helps ensure success as the parties go through the process of

- determining their shared purpose, goals, and accountabilities
- deciding how they will maintain two-way communication
- establishing outcomes
- setting up procedures for tracking, monitoring, and following up on their progress toward achieving successful results.

Partnering with Other Trainers

The training community is another source of opportunities for new and experienced practitioners to work together in partnership with other training professionals on a whole host of projects. These opportunities include

- providing leadership to training or other industry associations
- working on training projects outside the organization
- participating in pro bono and volunteer training work in the community.

These outside business partnerships provide trainers with opportunities to gain experience and expertise and to learn from one another, all the while providing them the chance to deliver services to their colleagues, clients, and the community. It also provides them with numerous occasions to increase their credibility as professionals both inside and outside of their organization.

For experienced trainers, the opportunity to work with their colleagues in the local chapter of ASTD on a project to produce an all-day, multisession training program for members, for example, is an excellent reason for entering a partnership. New practitioners often find it especially helpful to work closely with a local non-profit organization on a pro bono basis to help them resolve some of their particular training needs around such issues as supervision or team building. Volunteerism not only provides excellent opportunities for professional growth, but is also something that can go on the résumé of someone whose credentials need some "beefing" up.

THE REWARDS

Working in a strategic partnership or in a less formal relationship with your customers, external consultants, and colleagues offers rewards that extend beyond the successful completion of a project:

- A partnership allows each individual to be exposed to a wealth of information and knowledge possessed by the other parties, and this mutual learning enables all parties to achieve their goals together, while each profits from participating in an enriching, individual development experience.
- The nature of a partnership, with each party dependent on the other for success, often provides the individuals involved with the foundation for a

professional relationship that endures long after a project or initiative is completed.

- Working in partnership produces the best chance for all parties to succeed and with success comes the one thing that trainers value most—credibility.

You, too, can reap these benefits by becoming a more effective strategic partner. Take self-assessment 7-1 to learn how you can form more effective, strategic partnerships with your customers.

In Chapter 8, you will see how you can establish credibility in a hands-on way, that is, through improving your craft.

Self-Assessment 7-1.
Actions for becoming a more effective strategic partner.

1. On a scale of 1 to 10, with 10 being the highest, rate how effective your strategic partnerships are with your customers.

Not effective at all				Somewhat effective				Highly effective	
1	2	3	4	5	6	7	8	9	10

2. If you scored yourself 7 or below, begin to think about what you need to do to form more effective strategic partnerships with your customers. What immediate actions can you take to begin this process?

☐ Action: _____
☐ Action: _____
☐ Action: _____

3. On a scale of 1 to 10, with 10 being the highest, rate your organization in terms of the value it places on employees working cooperatively with one another, as well as with others who have a stake in its success.

No value				Somewhat valued				Valued highly	
1	2	3	4	5	6	7	8	9	10

4. If you scored your organization 7 or below, begin to think about what you can do to encourage people in your organization to work more cooperatively. What immediate actions can you take to begin this process?

☐ Action: _____
☐ Action: _____
☐ Action: _____

5. How successful have you been in establishing partnerships with professionals outside your organization? What actions can you take to improve the quality of these relationships?

☐ Action: _____
☐ Action: _____
☐ Action: _____

6. How would you describe the nature of your relationships with external consultants and vendors? What immediate actions can you take to move these relationships to partnerships?

☐ Action: _____
☐ Action: _____
☐ Action: _____

Self-Assessment 7-1.
Actions for becoming a more effective strategic partner (continued).

7. What immediate actions can you take that involve partnerships with customers, consultants, colleagues, and community members that will help you in your professional development?

☐ Action: _____

☐ Action: _____

☐ Action: _____

8

Improving Your Craft

"My belief is that an organization is a composite of its individual
members. The real values of the organization, the values that form
a company's character and ethics, and give depth, meaning, and
strength to its informal operating systems, are the values of its
members" (Weisbord, 1993).

 STRIVE FOR CREDIBILITY IN THE
CLASSROOM.

No book on trainer credibility would be complete without taking a look at the
trainer's role in ensuring a successful classroom training experience. This
role is clearly changing; more time is being spent providing consultative services to
customers in such areas as managing change and improving performance. But, to
not appreciate the importance of classroom training would be to deny much of the
work that trainers do today. The fact is that most of what a trainer does takes place
in the classroom. According to a national executive survey by ASTD (1998), "The
primary method for delivering leadership training [a category that includes training for nonsupervisory personnel all the way to executive-level employees] continued to be instructor-led, classroom courses." According to the survey, "Classroom-
based leadership training for middle-management was used by almost all organizations (96 percent) that offered formal leadership development opportunities,"
despite the growing use of technology-based learning methods, such as computer-
based training, teleconferencing, and intra- and Internet training tools.

MORE THAN JUST SKILLS AND TECHNIQUES

Credibility in the classroom is tied to many things. Naturally, trainers must know
and fully understand the subject they are presenting. They must also possess certain skills and techniques—conducting role plays, making eye contact with the
audience, and facilitating discussions, for example—so that they can help guide
participants through the training process to achieve a program's learning and per-

formance objectives. Nevertheless, a trainer's credibility depends on more than just skills and techniques or even the ability to make good presentations. Trainers begin to establish credibility even before they set foot in their classroom. For trainers, credibility starts with what they believe in, the values they hold true, and their attitude and thinking related to the learners, their organization, and the training experience as a whole.

To be credible, a trainer must be mentally and intellectually prepared to work with the learners to provide a learning experience that helps ensure the achievement of the program's overall objectives, while recognizing and respecting each member's needs. This means that while in the classroom trainers must use their power to influence in a positive way, encouraging people to follow them through their actions, behaviors, and words. They must do this all the while staying focused on their organization's mission so that they can provide the learners with the most relevant and meaningful training experience to support them in helping achieve their organization's strategic goals. To be able to do this, a trainer must first gain the learners' trust by being perceived as credible. The following sections describe five ways that a trainer can begin to do this.

Be Honest With the Learners

A trainer's credibility is continually being tested by the learners in the classroom: "Is this person telling the truth and being honest with me or is he or she just feeding me the company line?" and "Will this person provide an experience that will help in my development and give me what I need to perform in my job effectively?" and "Will I be able to use anything I learn in this program when I get back to my job?" As they sit in the classroom, the learners often ask themselves and sometimes each other these questions about trust as they determine whether to believe that the individual standing in front of the room truly represents their organization's beliefs, values, and expectations for the future.

To gain the learners' trust and be perceived as credible, a trainer must first start with a self-evaluation, being aware that in the eyes of those sitting in the classroom the trainer personifies the expectations and values of the organization. This means that trainers must be able to accept and believe in what they are presenting before they can expect to be honest and truthful with the learners. To do this, they must reconcile, before they ever enter the classroom, any differences they may have with what they are about to present to the learners. The trainer has the responsibility to raise the issue of anything he or she finds especially objectionable in the program with a manager or the customer to determine the best resolution before the training occurs.

If trainers feel strongly about a particular component in the program, they should also use their power to influence to persuade and educate those who have the authority to make changes. Trainers must be able to stand behind and support what they present to the learners in an honest and truthful fashion if they are to be perceived as credible. No trainer should ever say, "They said I'm supposed to say that the company wants every manager interviewed by three different people, but nobody really does that." As far as the audience is concerned, "they" and the trainer are the same entity. Even in the rare instance when trainers feel a strong need to express views that may be perceived as counter to the organization's thinking, they should do so in an open and honest fashion and state it as an opinion but never in a way that undermines the objectives of the program. As trainers come to terms with their own needs for honesty and truthfulness, it is important to extend these principles to all their interactions with the learners.

Although learners do not expect trainers to know everything, they do expect them to be forthright and truthful at all times especially about what they know and what they do not know. Because of their power to influence, trainers should be especially careful never to mislead the learners or misrepresent the organization. Trainers must recognize that they gain more credibility with the learners by acknowledging that they do not know the answer to a question than they do by trying to fake their way through it. This also holds true when the trainer is using a facilitator's guide or other company materials to conduct the program. For example, when a trainer knows that something in the material is wrong, has changed, or is outdated, he or she must take responsibility for obtaining and presenting the correct information; to do otherwise would threaten the integrity of the program and destroy the trainer's credibility. In every case, what makes trainers credible is not whether they know everything there is to know but rather the strength of their commitment to resolve as quickly as possible any learner's question that remains.

Put the Learners' Needs First

Just like talk show hosts who give flawless monologues night after night or like some management gurus who command $50,000 for presentations that teach managers how to become better leaders, trainers, too, must understand their audiences and put their needs first. Jay Leno knows what he needs to do so that his audience will laugh, and so, too, must a trainer know what the learners need so that they can perform more effectively after they return to work. Trainers must learn as much as they can about who the learners are before the session even begins. For example, whenever possible, trainers should try to learn about the learners' ranges of experience and levels of education, their job titles or the work they perform, and, most important, the kinds of pressing issues they confront on the job. Even when this information is not readily available, trainers can often obtain it by asking the people who would most likely know: the learners' managers, HR representatives, training colleagues, and, once the session begins, the learners themselves. Once they obtain this information, trainers can then use it to help direct the program along the appropriate path to meet the specific needs of the learners and achieve the program objectives.

Sometimes a trainer is drawn into a situation where it is necessary to try to satisfy two somewhat different needs at the same time. This can happen when a trainer is responsible for providing training for an ongoing, organization-wide program or initiative requiring him or her to present a consistent message to everyone in each program. This can present a challenge, because the trainer must sometimes balance the learners' needs against the organization's requirements for the training.

Consider, for example, the situation of the trainer in a large, national, managed-services company, headquartered in the northeastern United States, who was conducting her organization's midlevel-manager training program in different parts of the country. During the session on professionalism, the organization wanted it stressed that the appropriate dress for men was suits and ties and for women, business suits or dresses. Yet, every time the trainer went to the West Coast region, managers told her that this kind of dress was not appropriate in dealing with their customers and that in their part of the country they dressed more casually. Unfortunately, back east in the corporate office, the message to all employees continued to be suits, ties, and dresses. Although she could have easily avoided the issue and just left things as they were, the trainer realized that to continue to ask people to perform in a way that was counter to what made good business sense would be inappropriate. Upon arriving home after her last trip she contacted her manager, explained the situation, and asked him to lobby to get this part of the program changed to reflect the regional differences in appropriate dress. After some convincing, she and her manager were able to get the "rule" changed. This modification allowed her to provide a more meaningful training experience and, as word spread of her involvement in the issue, helped her establish a more credible relationship with her audiences on the West Coast.

To resolve such issues and maintain credibility, a trainer must possess working knowledge of the company and industry, and know that what he or she is presenting will help achieve the goals of the program, the organization, and the learners. In this case, the trainer had a good sense of the effect that enforcing this policy would have on the West Coast region's ability to meet sales goals. Maintaining the status quo would have resulted in frustrated employees and loss of potential sales. She also understood that to simply tell her audience not to pay attention to the rule could compromise her position with her superiors back east. She chose instead to get involved and take responsibility to get the rule changed. By doing this, she accommodated the needs of her audience, helped her organization keep up-to-date with business practices on the West Coast, and enhanced her credibility with all her customers.

Be Prepared

What trainers do to prepare to conduct a training program really depends on their experience, their comfort level with the material, and their personal style. Of course, for any trainer nothing beats practice, practice, and more practice. No matter how trainers prepare, though, once inside the classroom their level of preparedness influences their credibility in the eyes of the learners. At the very least, every trainer should be prepared to act on the following basic requirements:

- Understand and articulate the program's objectives and their connection to achieving the organization's overall objectives.
- Establish a classroom environment that promotes optimal learning.
- Use all program resources and materials in the way they were designed.
- Execute each component of the program, including lectures, discussions, and individual and group exercises, to achieve the program's objectives.

Trainers must sometimes do things outside the normal boundaries of their work and take their level of preparation beyond the basics. No doubt you have observed situations in which an otherwise competent trainer failed to recover after being thrown off by a question or situation for which he or she was unprepared. Unfortunately, a trainer who is so scripted is a bit like those little robots that deliver office mail; everything is fine until someone moves a desk, disrupting the programmed route.

To be perceived as credible and gain the learners' trust, a trainer must not only prepare for what is expected, he or she must also prepare for the unexpected. One way a trainer does this is through anticipation—thinking of questions, situations, issues, and problems that may come up at any point in the program. For example, although many trainers prepare by writing down their responses to questions that are a part of the program, a trainer can achieve real credibility by taking this practice one step further and also preparing responses for questions or issues that may arise but are not part of the training. These could include questions germane to the program itself or in some cases having to do with a sensitive local issue, say, a rumored layoff or some recent negative publicity about the company. In every case, the more aware the trainer is about what is happening in the organization, the easier it is to prepare for the pressing questions and issues that are on the minds of the learners. Trainers achieve credibility in the classroom and ensure a successful program when they anticipate the unexpected and are able to demonstrate flexibility in responding to the learners' individual needs.

A trainer also gains credibility by preparing relevant anecdotes, metaphors, stories, and examples to share with the learners that help reinforce or clarify a point. Building a repertoire to draw upon not only helps keep each program fresh for the audience but helps the trainer stay energized, too. For example, one trainer likes to tell the story of her company's senior vice president who climbed the corporate ladder to his present position after starting as an assistant manager at a store in Kansas. She tells this very compelling story during supervisory skills training as a way of illustrating how her company's succession planning process really works. Another very clever trainer collected interview "horror stories" that he would share with his audiences in the behavioral interviewing workshops that he conducted for every manager in his organization. These short anecdotes never failed to get the audience's attention and were frequently mentioned in the trainer's evaluations as especially helpful in reminding the managers about what not to do while conducting an interview.

One other way a trainer can achieve credibility with the learners is how he or she prepares the physical environment for the learning event. As one 20-year veteran trainer says, "Treat people coming into your classroom as if they are entering your living room." Trainers achieve credibility with the learners by paying close attention and taking time to prepare for the logistical end of the training experience. Whenever possible, especially when conducting training at an unfamiliar location, such as a hotel, a conference room, or even a seldom-used room at the company, trainers should make a point of visiting the classroom at least one hour before the event begins. This gives them the opportunity to get a feel for the space by doing a mental walkthrough, visualizing the various segments of the training program. It also allows them time to set an environment to give the learners the freedom to participate and the comfort to learn. Credible trainers pay attention to small details, such as deciding where to stand so that the learners can see and hear them, ensuring that the flipchart has enough paper, or learning how to turn the proper lights on and off after a PowerPoint presentation. The fact is that perceptions are important, and most audiences want trainers who know what they are doing and, at the very least, look like they have done such presentations before.

Be Respectful of Others

To gain their trust and be perceived as credible, trainers must be respectful of the learners by valuing the diversity of people and their ideas, while ensuring the needs of the group as a whole are satisfied. For example, trainers who are credible know the importance of establishing an atmosphere of mutual respect in the way they treat people even as they walk into the classroom before the program begins. An excellent way to set this tone is to acknowledge each individual as he or she enters the room, shake hands, and offer a personal greeting always using first names. Remember, trainers, in most cases, are automatically afforded a certain degree of power and respect by the learners just by their position. Trainers gain credibility when they use this power in a way that creates an environment of mutual respect, showing the learners that they can be trusted and making everyone feel comfortable. One seasoned professional tells a story about going to his first training program when he was new to the field. He was impressed by a trainer who went out of his way to shake hands and introduce himself to all 20 people who entered the program. He decided shortly afterward to become a trainer himself and has made it a point to carry on this practice with each person entering his own classroom. The trainer, to this day, is always amazed at the reaction he gets as people file into the room, because most are clearly not accustomed to being treated with such respect. He is convinced that his credibility with all his audiences begins at the point of that first contact—a handshake.

Of course, every trainer knows that the atmosphere in a classroom can quickly disintegrate if the trainer is not also paying attention to the continually changing conditions that exist within it. That is why it is important for the trainer to deal quickly with individuals who demonstrate a lack of respect for others in the classroom through inappropriate behaviors. Such behaviors—carrying on side conversations, interrupting class discussions, or returning late from breaks—often disrupt the flow of the program and can test the trainer's credibility with the learners as they look to see how the trainer will respond.

To maintain credibility in these situations, the trainer must act. Often what works best initially is to remind the class of what constitutes appropriate behavior without openly embarrassing any of the offending parties, for example, reminding the learners about limiting breaks to 10 minutes. This expresses to the audience that the trainer is aware of what is happening and that the trainer expects all inappropriate behaviors to stop. If the behaviors continue, the trainer must find an appropriate time, perhaps during a break in the program, to discuss the situation with those who have continued to flaunt the rules. This step is necessary to resolve the issue and maintain credibility with the rest of the class. Generally, this should be done in private to respect the self-esteem of the individuals involved and, by the end, the involved parties should be able to agree that the behavior will stop. Trainers gain credibility in the eyes of the learners when they use their power to influence, in this case to deal with disruptive behavior, in a constructive way that respects each individual, while benefiting the group as a whole.

Make Learning Enjoyable and Fun

Most trainers recognize that the learners will retain more in an environment where learning is enjoyable and fun. The challenge, however, is to do this and still maintain credibility. Some trainers are able to incorporate these elements into their programs, but others have difficulty pulling this off. They come off looking stilted and forced. When this happens, they begin to lose their credibility as the learners become more uncomfortable and start questioning the sincerity of the trainer.

Unfortunately, being spontaneous, entertaining, and humorous cannot be taught, but you can take actions to help ensure an enjoyable and fun training experience, while further establishing your credibility with the learners. You can start by taking an introspective look at what makes learning enjoyable and fun for the learners. If, for example, they enjoy frequent class discussions, games, or props, then try incorporating more of these activities in your training, always recognizing that the learners' needs should come first. Of course, you should also realize that if your attempts at humor usually result in blank stares from the learners, maybe you should save the jokes for your close friends and not use them in the classroom. Remember:

- Always be yourself; do not try to mimic or impersonate others.
- You should develop an individual style that is both audience-centered and compatible with who you are.
- Take your role as a trainer seriously, but do not take yourself too seriously.

One good way for you to develop a style of your own is through observing others and picking and choosing the behaviors and techniques of those you admire the most. This can include other trainers, as well as entertainers, politicians, religious leaders, and anyone else who gives frequent presentations to groups. You can then select the actions you are most comfortable with, try them out with the learners, and keep those that meet the test of being both audience-centered and compatible with the person you are. Another way is to do what one training consultant does at all his programs. He calls it "collecting friends." During breaks in his program, he goes around checking with different people in the audience on a one-to-one basis to get a sense of how the program is going and what he can do to improve it. Naturally, this takes a strong ego and a good deal of self-confidence. He finds, though, that his audiences truly appreciate his taking time to even ask them. Moreover, much of what he has incorporated into his style of training comes from these discussions with his "friends" in the class.

Trainers must know that they set the tone for their programs by how they behave and act in front of the learners. If you want a relaxed atmosphere that is more conducive to learning, you must make it happen. Trainers who have achieved credibility with the learners recognize the power of a smile and a sense of humor in helping remove any barriers to learning. Everything else being equal, trainers who enjoy what they are doing and make learning fun for the learners are more effective at what they do.

WHAT TRAINERS NEED

Credibility in the classroom is something you must strive for and work at, because it does not come automatically with the role. Successful classroom trainers are those able to incorporate the physical aspects of training—subject knowledge, training skills, and techniques—with the mental and emotional parts—how trainers approach their craft and the learners. Traditionally trainers have concentrated their efforts on developing the physical aspect of training rather than the mental and emotional parts. Unfortunately, a trainer who believes that success is a just a matter of mastering the content of each program and delivering it flawlessly is like a weightlifter who hopes to become a champion by working only his upper body and ignoring his legs. In either case, things are out of balance. Self-assessment 8-1 can help you focus on the mental and emotional aspects of training and suggests some actions you can take to improve your craft.

The problem with the overemphasis on improving skills and techniques is that it equates a trainer's craft with that of being a tactician. Trainers do not have to be the most polished performers to be successful because great theater does not always make for great training. What a trainer does need, though, is to be honest and respectful of others and always prepared. Trainers need to enjoy what they are doing, share this joy with others, and always put the learners first. Above all, trainers need to be credible.

Chapter 9 explores the process of becoming a credible training leader.

Self-Assessment 8-1.
Actions you can take to begin to improve your craft.

1. On a scale of 1 to 10, with 10 being the highest, rate your credibility in general with learners in the classroom.

Not credible				Somewhat credible				Very credible	
1	2	3	4	5	6	7	8	9	10

2. If you scored yourself 7 or below, begin to think about what you need to change to alter the learners' perceptions of your credibility. What immediate actions can you take to begin this process?

☐ Action: _____
☐ Action: _____
☐ Action: _____

3. What do you do to put the learners' needs first? How effective are you in doing this? What actions can you take to ensure that the learners' needs are paramount?

☐ Action: _____
☐ Action: _____
☐ Action: _____

4. What do you do to prepare for each program you conduct? What areas do you need to focus more attention on in your preparation? What immediate actions can you take to start this process?

☐ Action: _____
☐ Action: _____
☐ Action: _____

5. How do you define respect in the classroom? What do you do to ensure that mutual respect is always present? What actions can you take to start this process?

☐ Action: _____
☐ Action: _____
☐ Action: _____

6. What makes training and learning fun and enjoyable for you? Are these things compatible with being learner-centered? What do you try to incorporate into your programs to ensure an enjoyable atmosphere for everyone? What immediate actions can you take to start this process?

☐ Action: _____
☐ Action: _____
☐ Action: _____

9

Being a
Training Leader

"A simple charge for leadership that fulfills the goal of turning aspirations into actions, based on the defined assumptions, comes from the concept *credibility × capability*. Successful leaders of the future must be personally credible" (Ulrich, 1996).

 EXTEND YOUR INFLUENCE BEYOND THE CLASSROOM INTO THE OPERATING CORE OF THE ORGANIZATION.

Enough has been written about leadership to fill a small library. Bennis and Nanus (1985) point to the fact that decades of academic research have resulted in over 350 definitions of leadership and that was in 1985! The business world has been introduced to visionary leadership and transformational leadership; it has been taught that leadership is sometimes a science and other times an art; and it has been taught that some leaders are born, while others must learn to be leaders. Because all these theories and definitions point to one thing—that there is no simple explanation for leadership—it is safe to say that the search for these truths will go on long after the publication of this book.

Along these same lines, there is no one leadership style or set of traits indigenous to trainers, so to suggest that one way of being a training leader is any better or worse than another would be misleading at best. Nevertheless, trainers who are perceived as credible leaders in their organizations often demonstrate certain kinds of behaviors and conduct themselves in ways that enable them to provide leadership to their various stakeholders, while helping their organizations achieve their goals. Although all trainers possess to varying degrees the capacity to express their leadership and should do so when appropriate, usually the role of training leader is reserved for the titular head of the department. This person is generally regarded as having both responsibility and accountability for all training that occurs in the organization and also serves as its primary spokesperson and representative. Having this position and this title does not automatically confer credibility or leadership ability, however. Credibility and leadership come with having the right message, believing in it, and presenting it in a way that holds people's attention and leads them to take action that supports their organization in achieving its goals.

THE TRAINER'S ROLE IS A PARADOX

Interestingly, the trainer's role as it relates to leadership is somewhat of a paradox. Traditionally, this role has been primarily an instructional one, because trainers have often provided much of the learning involved in the development of new and experienced leaders in their organizations. Ironically, though, over the years few trainers, even those who are actually involved in training and developing leaders, have consistently exhibited the kind of leadership in their own work that they espouse in the classroom. Even worse, many training directors and managers do not even consider themselves leaders in their own organizations; they cannot see a connection between training, learning, and leading. Unfortunately, this dissonance between what trainers do and how they view themselves has sometimes resulted in a questioning of their credibility by those who would have a stake in their success.

The lack of historical precedents has often made the challenge for trainers wanting to exercise their capacity for leadership in their organizations a daunting one. Yet to be perceived as credible, trainers must take responsibility for advancing their profession from that of full-time program developers and deliverers to one focused on providing a wider range of services to improve performance, increase productivity, and support employee development, while helping achieve the organization's goals. To do this requires trainers, in general, to assume more of a leadership role in their organizations in helping to broaden the perception of training's value beyond the traditional classroom walls and into the operating core of the organization. Although this may not be a role traditionally assumed by trainers, it is certainly not inconsistent with the role that more trainers are beginning to play today as they seek to achieve greater credibility in their organizations.

HOW TO EXPRESS CAPACITY FOR LEADERSHIP

Trainers can express their capacity for leadership in two ways, as it relates to
- the organization and its people
- those with whom they have a managerial relationship and for whom they are responsible.

In both cases, the training leader sets the tone and is a driving force for his or her organization to achieve success through training. Training leaders can do this by
- defining the value of their service for the organization
- expressing their vision of the future
- leading by example
- being agents for change
- showing courage
- providing uncommon support to those they manage.

Defining the Value of Their Service for the Organization

Training leaders must define the value of their service to the organization and their customers. To do this, they must be able to explain who they are and who else comprises the training enterprise, what the training enterprise can do for the organization and their customers, what results their customers can expect, and how they will accomplish those results.

Although the answers to these questions are often addressed in the department's mission statement, core values, or marketing materials, it is important that they also be part of a continuous process that educates and enlightens people in their organization to how the training enterprise and the role of the trainer are connected with helping satisfy customer needs. In many instances, training leaders define the value of their service through words, actions, and behaviors that occur every day during the course of work. What helps make them credible, though, is their ability to articulate and model the behaviors that express this value in such a way that encourages the many stakeholders in their organization to follow and take action.

One way training leaders can define the value of their service for their customers is by constructing a variation of what many external consultants refer to as their "commercial message." A training leader's commercial message is a prepared statement offered to an individual or group that usually answers such questions as "Can you tell me what you and the training department do?" or "What can you and the training department do to help me?"

The training leader's commercial message consists of several basic elements that address the issues of who, what, how, where, and when. To effectively establish the value of the training leader's service, it is important that the message be clear, concise, and intelligible, although it does not necessarily have to include each element or be in a particular order. In fact in some cases it may even contain a response to when and where trainers do what they do. The following is an example of a commercial message. . . .

- (Who) "I'm Jean Arons, the director of training. I work with a highly qualified and diverse team of three other trainers. Together we have 50 years' experience in both training and operations in our industry. In fact, two of our trainers, whom you may know, were assistant managers in our southern region."

- (What) "We provide a wide range of training services designed to improve employee performance, as well as help people develop personally and professionally. Our focus is on obtaining measurable results that help achieve both employee and organizational goals. For example, you may be aware that we recently helped our information technology department significantly improve service to their internal customers. We did this by determining that the major issue in meeting their customer needs had to do with managing their time effectively. We made some changes in the way they responded to calls and offered some training that has produced a 50 percent improvement in their customer service ratings in less than four months."

- (How) "We like to work in partnership with our customers so that we can best meet their needs. That means we like to start by meeting with you and perhaps even others who have a stake in your success to really determine what your specific needs are so that we can help provide the most appropriate response. We provide our services in many different settings."
- (Where) "Most think we just do classroom training, however, in the case of the information technology training, for example, we did most of the training on site."
- (When) "Because of our experience and expertise, we are often able to provide services on a just-in-time basis, which can really save time and money."

A training leader's commercial message is not a speech to be read verbatim. It is also safe to say that every commercial message is different and specific to the training leader's message, style, and language. In a situation where the work of the training leader and the training enterprise is known within the organization, the message may be reserved primarily for new people coming into the organization. In any case, it is meant to serve as a talking point to help the training leader explain briefly the training services and the value added by helping to meet the customers' and potential customers' needs. Training leaders, however, are not the only ones who should have a commercial message ready for use. All trainers should be prepared at all times to discuss the services they provide and the value these services add in helping meet their customers' needs and achieve their organization's goals. Although their message may be somewhat different from the training leader's, it should consist of, at the very least, the same basic elements of who, what, how, where, and when.

For the commercial message to convey effectively the value of training services, it is important that it

- be brief, usually no more than two to three minutes long
- be stated using the training leader's own words and style and in terms that are consistent with the relationship he or she has with the individual or group he or she is speaking to, as well as the situation in which it is being said
- be focused on what adds value for the particular customer or customers being addressed
- excite people to use his or her services
- headline the benefits and results of the services up front
- help establish the training leader and his or her colleagues as credible resources for the organization.

Expressing Their Vision for the Future

Many businesses have written a vision statement that expresses what the organization wants to be in the future. Depending on the company and its leadership, these statements often give meaning to what the future will look like for the organization and its people. In a similar way, training leaders, to be credible, should also be able to express to their many stakeholders how they would like the training enterprise to look in the future. They can begin doing this by creating a picture of the future through words that inspire their training colleagues and others in their organization to take part in helping realize the vision. To start, training leaders must express their vision of the future, aligned with what has been expressed by the organization's senior leader, in a way that clearly frames training's role in supporting the organization and its people to achieve their goals. The vision must be more than simply an idea; it should project the ideal of the future, an emotional expression of the training leader's commitment. It should be ambitious in scope and able to move people to action. One training leader in a midsize company, for example, set a course to realize his vision of a full curriculum of courses that can be offered to departments and business units on a just-in-time basis. Another training leader envisions using her company's intranet to provide training on a whole host of subjects to any employee, anywhere.

Naturally it is not enough to simply have a vision of what the ideal future will be like. The training leader must be able to mobilize forces and direct efforts to realize the vision. This requires credible leadership to bring people together, obtain the necessary resources, and instill commitment in all involved in helping it succeed. It must start, though, with everyone who has a stake in its success having the same picture in his or her mind that gives a sense of destiny. As for the training leader looking to create this vision of the future, it is helpful to not get caught up with issues of structure and style. What is more important is the passion behind the will to realize the vision than the formality of its conception or the eloquence in which it is stated.

[handwritten margin note: TO ASK UP TRAINERS EVERYWHERE TO COMMIT TO PERSUING & REALIZING M P I]

Leading by Example

Credible leaders recognize the power of perception and the importance of leading by example. This is very true for training leaders who are often put in a position of having to put their money where their mouth is. For example, consider what happened at a small regional bank that implemented a complex performance management system throughout the organization. The training director was the champion for the project that required almost six months to put in place. In fact, most managers at the bank considered the director's leadership to be the most important factor in getting everyone's buy-in to making the system work, as well as getting people truly excited about using it.

However, six months after the rollout of the program, word leaked out from her own department that the training director, who was now being viewed as a rising star, had failed to conduct any performance planning meetings, an important first step in the process, with her own staff. Needless to say the training director's credibility took a significant hit as some long-time employees started to complain about how this was just another in a long line of "flavor-of-the month" programs at the bank. Even worse, as word spread about the training director's seeming lack of commitment, other managers, despite their earlier endorsements, began to question whether it was worth all the time and effort to put the system into their departments. Ultimately, the system failed and was eventually discarded because its champion, her credibility irreparably harmed, could no longer rally support for it.

Because of their power to influence, training leaders must understand that those they provide services to often take their cues from the trainer in determining the importance of following through on any training-sponsored initiative. Perhaps no greater example of this is the issue of continual employee learning mentioned in chapter 6. A training leader who does not expand his or her own learning and development cannot possibly expect others to advocate and support the idea of continual employee learning as a company value. In situations like these, where the training leader is sending conflicting messages to those he or she wishes to influence, the end result is often a loss of credibility that makes championing any new training initiative difficult at very best.

Being Agents for Change

Some would say the term that best describes the business world in the last decade is *change*. Although today the term has become somewhat commonplace, the issues of change and how to stay on top of it continue to be important ones for most organizations. Traditionally many trainers have taken a more passive role in helping their organizations through the process of what is often referred to as managing change. The trainer's role has usually involved producing and conducting so-called change management programs. Of course, anyone who has ever had to sit through one of these programs knows that most of them have had little effect on easing the change process for employees and even less on ways of managing it.

With change now the norm for most organizations, the training leader's role has shifted from supplier of change programs to change agent. As a change agent, the training leader must now take a more active role in helping his or her organization navigate through the unsettling effect of change and especially the effect it has on people. To do this requires the training leader to be active in searching out new opportunities for applying training solutions to the issues and problems brought about by constant change. The following are 10 ways that training leaders can use their power to influence to be a change agent in their organization:

1. Start by adjusting their own attitudes toward change, embracing it as an opportunity for growth and then translating this thinking into meaningful action that serves as a model for others.

2. Help develop and implement a communication strategy with senior leadership that includes provisions for informing all employees why a change is taking place, where the organization is headed, and what role they will play in helping it get there.

3. Conduct informal surveys of their customers to assess their reaction to organizational changes and then develop and implement a strategy with senior leadership to address the issues that come up most frequently.

4. Be an advocate for change by taking risks and acting innovatively and modeling the behaviors that help generate enthusiasm, commitment, and action throughout the organization.

5. Research and recommend to senior leadership new methods for delivering training (for example, computer-based training) that more appropriately responds to the changing needs of the organization.

6. Assess which new skills and training employees need to meet the demands of the organization's changing future; develop and implement a strategy to address these needs.

7. Assess what cultural norms (for example, poor communication between staff in the corporate office and operators in the field) are creating roadblocks to change and develop and implement with senior leadership a strategy to eliminate them.

8. Develop and implement a strategy that removes any obstacles and makes it easy for people throughout the organization to receive training when and where it is most needed (for example, preparing more field trainers to deliver training).

9. Help others see the big picture by resisting the tendency toward entrenchment and encourage all who have a stake in the organization to work toward its common good during times of change.

10. Be a primary resource for senior leadership regarding organizational change and its effect on employees.

Showing Courage

How one responds in the face of adversity is perhaps the defining moment for a leader. Like most leaders, training leaders are presented with situations that test their credibility and require tough decisions. Although there are many opportunities for training leaders to demonstrate courage in the work they do, the following three examples stand out above the rest:

- the courage to admit they were wrong
- the courage to say no
- the courage to challenge the status quo.

To be credible, leaders must be able to recognize their mistakes and admit when they are wrong. This is certainly true for the training leader. Designing and developing appropriate training responses to needs that arise in an organization are not exact sciences. Despite the best assessment and planning, there are times when the solution chosen just does not fit the need. All too often, these situations are played out in public, especially when the training response is in the form of a training program or large-scale initiative. Training leaders gain credibility, however, when they use these times of adversity as opportunities for learning and exhibit the confidence to move on and try again, realizing that the self-assuredness they exhibit has a lot to do with how they are perceived in the future.

The training leader also must have the courage to say no. Not every request for training requires a training response. The training leader, though, has a greater responsibility than simply maintaining credibility in individual situations with departments or business units. As the primary representative for training in the organization, the training leader must also have the courage to question decisions often made by senior leadership having to do with employee training and development that the training leader believes would not be in the best interest of the entire organization.

Of course saying no is not enough. The training leader must use his or her experience and expertise as a trainer and knowledge of the organization to offer reasonable alternatives. Take the example of the training leader in the midwest accounting firm who raised questions regarding the efficacy of a mentoring program that was being pushed by one of the senior partners. In the original proposal, little money and no real plan were laid out to support the program. The training leader who supported the idea conceptually made a convincing argument to the firm's leadership that he would run the program, but only if it were set up to succeed with the right financial support and the buy-in of the organization's leadership. With a little arm-twisting and some examples of how other companies instituted their mentoring programs, he received the verbal commitment and funding he needed and was able to design and implement a successful program. Needless to say, his credibility as a leader, illustrated by his courage to stand up for what he believed, served him well in the future as he was able to win support for some training initiatives for which he had long sought approval.

Challenging the status quo takes courage because it usually means leaving what is comfortable only to enter the great unknown. The training leader establishes credibility in the organization sometimes by being the voice of reason and sometimes being the voice of unreason. This, of course, is not to suggest that the training leader should make a habit of raising unreasonable requests, but rather that he or she should not yield to the temptations of complacency. More important, the training leader should not allow the organization to always settle for what is instead of what could be. The training leader has a responsibility regarding issues of employee training and development to keep abreast of both the research and current trends in the field, so that he or she can continually challenge the organization's thinking about how best to prepare its people to achieve its goals.

Many organizations operate on the premise that "if it's not broken, don't fix it." Training leaders, however, can opt to use their power to influence in ways that allow their thoughts and ideas about what they believe would be best for the common good to be heard by those in a position to establish policy and make decisions for the organization. One way to do this would be to ask for periodic meetings throughout the year with senior leadership to discuss issues directly affecting the organizations and possible ways that training could be used to address them. Another way would be to lobby for placement on important committees and task forces in order to influence outcomes in which training may play a role. A third way would be to use a training council previously mentioned in this book, as the means for taking a fresh look at the the way the training enterprise supports the organization. Finally, use any and all means to educate decision makers in your organization through books, articles, and the latest research about new ways of incorporating training into the overall company strategy.

Providing Uncommon Support to Those They Manage

Besides the leadership they provide around issues pertaining to training and development and its relationship to achieving organizational goals, most training leaders also have managerial responsibilities that include providing support to the employees who report to them. In this capacity training leaders are expected to perform the more common managerial duties like delegating work, providing the resources to do the work, and, at the end of the review period, evaluating the work of those they supervise. Although it is important that these responsibilities be carried out effectively and efficiently, what truly helps make training leaders credible is the more uncommon support they provide to those they manage. The following are some actions that training leaders can take to provide uncommon support:

- *Establish measurable performance goals.* If asked, most managers would acknowledge the importance of setting goals on an annual or periodic basis with those who report to them. The fact is, though, for many this process either gets pushed to the side as other responsibilities pile up or is relegated to a paper and pencil task done only for compliance reasons. Training leaders who are effective managers and credible do the uncommon and take establishing measurable performance goals with those they provide support to seriously, even when no formal system for doing so in their organization exists. What training leaders do that separates them from the others are the following five actions: (1) they set performance goals together with each person on their staff, allowing for maximum input from the employee; (2) they ensure that the goals are aligned with both the training enterprise and the organization's goals; (3) they ensure that the goals are written in terms that are clear and measurable; (4) they set up a plan for monitoring the achievement of the goals and step in to provide coaching and support when the employee is having difficulty staying on track; and (5) they recognize the achievement when goals are achieved.

- *Empower employees to make decisions.* Establishing measurable performance goals is a first step toward empowering employees, because it helps clarify both parties' expectations about what their roles will be in ensuring the employee's success in doing their work. This helps reduce the two biggest impediments to empowerment: a manager feeling a loss of control and his or her lack of trust that the employee is able to do what needs to be done to get the work completed. A good place for the training leader to start is by empowering his or her employees to work directly with the customers. This means ensuring that all trainers on staff are knowledgeable about the mission and goals of the training enterprise, are clear about how the goals of the training enterprise mesh with those of the organization, and are prepared to serve their customers in ways that are aligned with both the organization and the training enterprise. The reason for doing this is clear; most trainers provide better customer service when they are responsible and held accountable for satisfying their customer's needs than when they are not.

- *Coach employees.* Coaching is a relationship between a manager and employee by which they work together to help employees improve their levels of performance. Training leaders often provide coaching to employees in two situations: coaching for development and coaching to improve performance. In the first instance, the coach and employee work together to gain a shared understanding of the employee's development needs and construct a plan to help the employee achieve personal and professional goals. In the second instance—coaching to improve performance—the coach and employee work together to gain a shared understanding of a performance problem and then together identify alternative solutions and agree to a specific plan to resolve the problem. Training leaders gain credibility by incorporating coaching into their everyday style of management. This is often demonstrated in their liberal use of such skills as active listening, giving and asking for feedback, effective questioning, and showing empathy.

- *Encourage teamwork.* Training leaders who are effective managers recognize the power of teamwork and encourage those who report to them to work together to help their customers achieve their goals. Whether individuals are working as a formal team or simply helping their colleagues, training leaders, by their actions, can promote and support their people working together in a number of ways: (1) assigning work that requires interdependency among staff; (2) providing each person with the resources to contribute to the team's work; (3) modeling the behaviors expected in team members; (4) being a resource and coach if and when the team falters; (5) rewarding people for working together; and (6) celebrating team successes.

- *Debrief after every failure and success.* Kouzes and Posner (1995b) underscore the importance of team debriefing at the end of and even during a project to capture the lessons learned and improve their efforts in the future. Of course, training leaders should make debriefing sessions a standard part of the way they conduct their business when dealing with teams, as well as with staff members who may be working on a project independently. Kouzes and Posner recommend posing some questions as part of the debriefing: "What did we do well?" "What did we do poorly?" "What did we learn from this?" and "How can we do better the next time?" In addition, the training leader should ask the questions of himself or herself by substituting "I" for "we" in the questions. When debriefing becomes a normal part of doing business, any threat that trainers might feel when they discuss situations that did not turn out the way they would have liked are lessened. This, of course, helps lead to a more accurate analysis of each project and the opportunity to make the right kinds of improvements for the future.

- *Make recognition public.* Most trainers understand the importance of incorporating various forms of recognition into the training activities they develop and produce for their customer, because recognition is an excellent motivator. Yet some training managers seem to be less aware of recognition's beneficial effect on their own staff members. Recognizing the accomplishments of those who participate in their organization's training activities and those who provide training services is part of what makes a training leader credible. In both instances, the key is making the recognition public. For example, in many companies employees who have completed training are recognized in the company newsletter. One enterprising training manager took this a step further by ensuring a spot on her company's quarterly management meeting agenda so that she could recognize training achievements made by employees in front of the entire management team. Training leaders find that public recognition of their staff members is a great confidence builder and motivator. One of the easiest ways to do this is placing a letter of commendation that goes right into an employee's personnel file. On the other end is the public recognition at the company's yearly HR meeting where trainers and others who have made special contributions are celebrated. Falling between these options are hundreds of ways that with a little creativity and forethought can provide the perfect incentive for trainers to excel in their work. Although some training leaders find that their time is often stretched with conducting "business," time taken to recognize the accomplishments of customers and staff should never be the part of their job that gets sacrificed.

CONTINUALLY SELF-ASSESS

Trainers become leaders based not only on what they do and how they relate and respond to others, but also based on who they are. This means continually reassessing their purpose, their goals, their values, their personal mission and vision, and the essence of who they are as a person and professional. Training leaders do this because of the value they place on their individual and spiritual growth and how their development as a person plays such an important part in their ability to lead others. Some do this by conducting their own mini-360-degree feedback sessions, continually asking peers, customers, their managers, and those who report to them to assess their performance and then use the feedback to develop a personal plan for improvement. Others take a more psychological approach and retreat to their own private place where they can take a more introspective look at themselves. No matter how they go about it, what is clear for training leaders, like all leaders, is that they must know themselves first before they can know and lead others. Self-assessment 9-1 lists some actions you can take to become an effective training leader in your organization.

Chapter 10 will explore the future of training and why it is important for trainers to focus on performance.

Self-Assessment 9-1.
Actions you can take to become an effective training leader in your organization.

1. On a scale of 1 to 10, with 10 being the highest, rate your capacity to provide leadership regarding the use of the training enterprise as a means of helping achieve organizational goals.

Weak leadership				Some leadership					Strong leader
1	2	3	4	5	6	7	8	9	10

2. On a scale of 1 to 10, with 10 being the highest, rate your capacity to provide leadership to those who report to you.

Weak leadership				Some leadership					Strong leader
1	2	3	4	5	6	7	8	9	10

3. If you scored 7 or below on either of the above, begin to think about some actions you can take to improve your ability and skill to provide leadership that inspires, motivates, and helps support the achievement of individual and organizational goals.

☐ Action: _____
☐ Action: _____
☐ Action: _____

4. Construct your own commercial message and try it out on your colleagues.

5. Ask your staff to construct their own commercial messages and provide feedback to them for improving it.

6. Begin to think about your vision for the training enterprise. What does it look like? Try testing it out with those you trust and ask for feedback.

7. In what ways have you been a change agent in your organization? What change issues are the most critical for your organization today? What actions can you and your colleagues take to help in this transition?

☐ Action: _____
☐ Action: _____
☐ Action: _____

8. What do leaders you admire seem to do particularly well? What can you take from them and incorporate into your own style?

9. What about your leadership style seems to work the best? What seems to cause problems in dealing with those who report to you? What actions can you take immediately to help change a negative situation to a positive?

☐ Action: _____
☐ Action: _____
☐ Action: _____

10

Where Training is Headed: Focus on Performance

"The foundation of the [human performance technology] HPT model is the analysis of human performance. Only through a rigorous analysis of people's performance in the workplace can we, as training professionals, select appropriate delivery strategies and technologies. Only through such analysis is it possible to create a highly competitive company of star performers" (Elliott, 1996).

 IN THE NEW WORLD OF HPI, TRAINERS FACE OPPORTUNITIES AND CHALLENGES.

Where is the field of training headed? What does the future look like for those who have been working in the field as trainers and for those new practitioners just embarking on their careers? As you have probably gathered by now from reading this book, the field of training and development continues to evolve as trainers build their credibility by exploring new, expanded approaches to help support their organizations in achieving its goals. A good place to find the answers to these questions and gain a sense of this evolution is the 1997 National HRD Executive Survey conducted by ASTD. The survey included responses provided by more than 300 HRD executives and managers who were asked to offer their view of what HRD trends they expected to see immediately (1997) and in the next three years (by 2000).

SURVEY RESULTS

In some ways, the results of the survey are rather predictable. For example, among the highly ranked needs were training on computer skills and teamwork, two areas that have almost become staples in American business. Perhaps the most intriguing finding, however, has to do with the top-ranking trend forecasted in the next three years: a "shift from providing 'training' to improving 'performance,'" something that has been mentioned throughout this book. (Because the survey showed results for 1997, this trend was actually a prediction for 2000.) According to the survey, those who responded "believe that HRD is undergoing a profound shift in its purpose. No longer is 'training' the primary deliverable of HRD. Instead, the emphasis has turned to its outcomes, especially performance and, somewhat less so, learning."

This new emphasis on improving performance is best illustrated by those involved with one of the performance-oriented approaches. Perhaps the most well known of these approaches is human performance improvement (HPI), also termed human performance technology (HPT). The roots of these performance-oriented technologies can be traced back to general systems theory, as well as the work of the influential behaviorist B.F. Skinner. Skinner used the term *operant conditioning* to explain how behavior increases in frequency the more it is reinforced or rewarded. Of course, the same is true for performance. More recent proponents of HPI and other performance-oriented approaches, including Thomas Gilbert, Joe Harless, Geary Rummler, Jim Fuller, and Dana and Jim Robinson, have focused attention on the issues of HPI in the workplace. In fact, much of the literature on the subject today either has been written by these individuals or is based on their work.

AUTHORS

Definitions of HPI abound in the literature, but perhaps the one that is most comprehensive, yet concise, reads thus: "a systemic and systematic approach to identifying the barriers that prevent people from achieving top performance, recognizing that top performance is key to an organization's success" (Sugrue & Fuller, 1999). Certainly, the important words here are *systemic* and *systematic*. Human performance interventions are systemic because all the variables with the system must be examined to determine what has an effect on performance. Each problem is viewed in the context of the entire system: "Unless all the components of the system are operating correctly, it will be impossible to optimize performance" (Fuller & Farrington, 1999). For example, training a group of employees to work more effectively as a team, but continuing to evaluate and reward them on an individual basis, would be a solution to a need that does not take into consideration the entire system and would probably fail in the long term.

Because HPI is a systematic approach, it follows an ordered set of steps to achieve results. A systematic approach ensures that no important factors are overlooked and that no hasty conclusions are drawn about the root causes of the barriers to performance. Unlike most training interventions, which usually take the form of events or activities such as a program or workshop, HPI is process-oriented. It consists of a series of actions that, when done successfully, delivers measurable results in terms of improved performance. In addition, HPI is usually a more cost-effective and efficient alternative to large-scale interventions, which often require a major investment of time and money for design, development, and implementation—an important consideration for most organizations.

THE ROLE OF PERFORMANCE CONSULTANT

Those who are practitioners of HPI or other performance-oriented approaches are often referred to by titles that suggest the work they do: performance improvement consultant, performance technologist, or human performance improvement consultant. The title that seems to be used most often when describing someone who focuses on helping the customers and the organization improve performance is *performance consultant.*

Robinson and Robinson (1995) differentiate between the role of performance consultant and the traditional trainer: "Someone in the role of performance consultant thinks in terms of what people must do if business goals are to be achieved. This is different from the traditional training process of focusing on what people must learn." According to the Robinsons, there are "four key areas of knowledge and skill needed if the performance consultant is to be successful:

- business knowledge
- knowledge of human performance technology
- partnering skill
- consultative skill."

Although it is true that this set of knowledge and skills differ from those associated with the traditional trainer, they are very similar to the knowledge and skills necessary to be what has been described in this book as a credible trainer (with the exception of knowledge of human performance technology). For example, both the performance consultant and credible trainer work to understand the organization and the industry in which it operates, including the organization's products and services, its competition, how it makes money, industry trends, and the outlook for the future. The performance consultant and credible trainer also work in partnership with their customers, creating relationships built on trust, respect, and two-way communication. Finally, each uses several effective consultative skills, such as listening and questioning, to identify the underlying issues affecting the performance problem to arrive at the appropriate interventions to help resolve them.

What exactly does a performance consultant do and how does he or she do it? The answer to these questions is "It depends." Because there are different approaches to improving performance, the performance consultant's work varies according to the situation, as well as to which approach the performance consultant ascribes. In addition, each performance problem often calls for more than one kind of intervention to help resolve it, so much of what the performance consultant does changes from project to project. Fuller and Farrington (1999) offer one relatively simple view of HPI and the role the performance consultant plays. They point to four major areas that are the focus of performance consultants as they deliver their service:

1. conducting analyses
2. establishing root causes
3. recommending and implementing solutions
4. evaluating results.

Conducting Analyses

In the analysis stage, the performance consultant and customer first determine exactly what the business needs are and decide upon the measures they will use to decide whether these needs have been satisfied. To do this effectively, the performance consultant must have a working knowledge of the customer's business, an understanding of the language of that business, and an awareness of the business issues within the context of the entire organizational system. The performance consultant then analyzes the business issue being considered, determines what performance is appropriate to resolve the problem, and identifies the performance gaps between what is happening and what should be happening.

Establishing Root Causes

The performance consultant, with the help of the customer, next seeks to determine the root causes of the performance gap. To discover the root causes, the performance consultant can select from several methods, ranging from fishbone diagrams, a method borrowed from the quality movement, to an approach that simply repeats the question "why?" again and again until the root causes of the performance gap have been identified. Another way the performance consultant may try to establish the root causes of the performance gap is by determining whether the gap is related to problems involving knowledge, skills, motivation, or environment. Once the performance consultant believes that the root causes are identified, he or she then goes about validating the findings, often through observation and, in some cases, by interviewing those with a stake in resolving the issue.

Recommending and Implementing Solutions

After the problem has been determined and the root cause identified and validated, the performance consultant, working with the customer, then recommends solutions that will remove the barriers to performance. These solutions can range from training interventions to construction of appropriate job descriptions to work redesign to changes in how employees are rewarded for doing their jobs. The performance consultant then decides who could best implement each of the interventions. For example, a performance consultant who is a former trainer may determine that training is one way to resolve the problem, and then design and implement a training workshop. If another type of solution is required, the performance consultant may opt to bring in professionals from the HR department or information technology, for example, to provide assistance with redesigning reward systems, developing more effective ways of retrieving information, or other appropriate interventions.

Evaluating Results

Typically the evaluation phase starts as far back as the initial analysis and continues throughout the HPI process. During this time, the performance consultant, working in conjunction with the customer, monitors the process to ensure that it is proceeding properly. After the interventions have been implemented, the performance consultant then takes the necessary steps to measure whether the goals have been achieved and whether the performance gaps have been closed. Depending on what was decided in the analysis phase, the performance consultant usually reviews the data produced during the process and compares it with the objectives established in the beginning. Of course, in many instances, the fruits of the performance consultants' work are not harvested until well after they are done. In these cases, the performance consultant must follow up later to ensure that the interventions were a success (Fuller & Farrington, 1999).

DOES THIS TREND SIGNAL THE END OF TRAINING?

The movement toward HPI raises some important questions for those in the training profession. If this trend toward a greater emphasis on performance is to be believed (and there is nothing to suggest otherwise), does this signal the end of the training profession as we know it? Where does this leave the many training professionals who have worked diligently over the years to serve their organizations and customers?

The answer to the first question is both no and yes. The training profession of today will still be around tomorrow, next week, and very likely in the years to come. Even most performance consultants acknowledge that if an organization wanted to move to an HPI approach, it would take anywhere from two to five years to gain acceptance and be put into place in most cases. As more new practitioners are exposed to different strategies and approaches, such as HPI and other, measurable interventions, traditional training will become one, but not the only, option from which trainers can choose to satisfy their customers' needs.

What must change for training to maintain its place as an effective means for organizations and their people to achieve their goals is the traditional view that training is the answer to every employee-related problem. Training is usually the right choice when the issue is either an employee's lack of knowledge or skill. However, as most people recognize, not all problems or issues fall into this category. When it comes to problems having to do with employee performance or motivation or organizational change, training, at least in the traditional sense, is rarely the best solution. In these instances, taking an HPI approach may be the better choice.

Where does this leave trainers, both seasoned professionals and those new to the field? Surprisingly, they are finding themselves in a world filled with opportunities and, not so surprisingly, they are anticipating a number of challenges ahead. Although training workshops and programs will remain an integral part of their repertoire, trainers in the future will establish credibility within their organization through the expanded services they will be able, and expected, to provide their customers. Traditional training is usually a very expensive proposition. Because developing and implementing training programs often costs thousands of dollars, organizations will look to more cost-effective and efficient ways to serve their employees' training, performance, and developmental needs. This means that trainers will spend less time in the classroom and more time closer to where the customer lives and works.

To be perceived as credible in the future, trainers must begin to change their thinking about training and the services they provide. This may be difficult for many trainers who have grown up, so to speak, and earned their reputations, by designing and conducting well-conceived and highly rated training programs. Nevertheless, a trainer's change in thinking does not necessarily mean a total change in the way he or she conducts business. This kind of change has more to do with inclusion than exclusion; that is, adding to the kinds of services trainers provide, rather than eliminating and starting all over. Some trainers may ask, "Will I need to stop calling myself a trainer and start calling myself a performance consultant?" This question puts the cart before the horse and, unfortunately, misses the point because titles in many organizations tend to be artificial; they rarely describe what a person really does. What is more important is not what the individual is called, but what the individual does and the value he or she brings to the customer.

How can trainers stay ahead of the many changes affecting the way they conduct their business and still provide the kinds of services that meet both their customers' and their organization's needs for achieving their goals? The following sections suggest some initial steps that will help trainers, both new and experienced, prepare for a future that is filled with opportunities and challenges. These ideas focus on expanding the kinds of services that trainers can provide for their customers in light of the trend toward HPI:

- *Learn about performance-oriented technologies.* The first step trainers should take is to learn as much as they can about human performance systems and, more specifically, the different performance-oriented technologies such as HPI. If this is truly the wave of the future, as most students of training believe, to dismiss it as nothing more than a passing fad would be to risk being left behind. An excellent place to start is by reading some of the literature on the subject. The Additional Resources section of this book and the References section list many useful books on HPI and training. Two books that should be on every trainer's list to read are *Performance Consulting: Moving Beyond Training* by Dana and James Robinson and *From Training to Performance Improvement: Navigating the Transition* by Jim Fuller and Jeanne Farrington. Each gives a detailed explanation of how the transition to performance improvement can help organizations achieve their goals. In a somewhat different vein, the book *In Action: Improving Performance in Organizations,* edited by William Rothwell and David Dubois, is a casebook of real examples of HPI interventions that have been conducted in a number of businesses.

- *Start small.* Learning about HPI will lead to the second action trainers can take. They can seek opportunities to incorporate a performance improvement approach into their current work within their own organizations. By starting with small projects, trainers can begin to establish credibility in their organizations by demonstrating their ability and willingness to tackle problems that fall outside of what they have typically involved themselves in while conducting classroom training. The list of opportunities could include helping a department provide better service to their internal customers to determining the reasons for and ways to prevent a team of managers from continually going over budget. Small projects allow trainers to practice what they have learned and gradually introduce to their organization a new set of services that they can provide.

- *Bring in other experts.* A third action trainers can take while working on some small performance improvement projects is encouraging others who work in their organization to join them in helping resolve some specific performance issues. Because HPI often involves multiple interventions, bringing in professionals from HR, finance, and information technology, when appropriate, is an excellent way to ensure the success of the project and create a cadre of performance improvement specialists for future interventions. As these teams of experts gain experience and develop a reputation for doing good work, more opportunities to use HPI interventions will arise, and the organization's leaders will learn that HPI is a reasonable option to deal with performance problems.

- *Spread the good news.* Finally, after a success or two, the fourth action that a trainer can take is to spread the word throughout the organization about the successful application of HPI. By publicizing their demonstrated successes, trainers can begin to pick up converts to the new services they are able to provide to their customers. As they continue to expand their range of services and involve others from the outside, trainers will be in a better position to increase their credibility within their organization, while satisfying their customers' needs more effectively and efficiently.

THINK, ACT, AND PERFORM DIFFERENTLY

As is the case with any change or movement away from a place of comfort, there is always some risk and some anxiety involved. The same is true for those in the training profession who are now recognizing the need to think, act, and perform in many new ways. Although tactical solutions, usually in the form of a training program or workshop, have been the norm for years, trainers must now consider the strategic implications of what they do and how they serve their customers and their organizations. Unfortunately for some, this realization has come too late and at the expense of trainers who have lost their jobs because they were the most logical choice to let go during times of downsizing and restructuring. After all, tactical solutions to ongoing problems rarely translate into bottom-line results.

For these reasons, the movement toward adopting new ways of satisfying their customers' needs and helping their organizations achieve their goals through approaches like HPI and other measurable interventions has brought new life to the training community. This phenomenon does not mean, however, that the long-recognized business of training and development no longer has value. What it does mean is a very definite change in the way trainers view and serve their customers, who now have more options than ever for meeting their needs.

The increased use of performance improvement approaches is just one example of how the field of training is changing. The choice for trainers is simple: Either remain open to new ways of meeting the demands of their customers or remain smug and steadfast in recommending training as the universal solution to every employee-related problem. To see how you are embracing the move toward HPI, take self-assessment 10-1. Remember that if training is to remain the primary means for helping prepare employees to meet the changing needs of the future, it, too, must change to reflect that future. Amidst all the change, there is but one constant for trainers who wish to serve their customers and their organizations for today and the years ahead: Be credible.

Now that you better understand the value of establishing credibility as a trainer, the final chapter will help you determine where you go from here so that you can take charge of your career.

Self-Assessment 10-1.
Actions you can take to meet your customers' future
performance improvement needs.

1. On a scale of 1 to 10, with 10 being the highest, rate your knowledge of HPI and how it can be used to meet customer needs in your organization.

    | | Somewhat | | Very |
    | Unfamiliar | knowledgeable | | knowledgeable |
    | 1 2 3 | 4 5 6 | 7 8 | 9 10 |

2. If you scored yourself 7 or below, begin to think about what you need to do to increase your knowledge of HPI. What immediate actions can you take to begin this process?

    ☐ Action: _____
    ☐ Action: _____
    ☐ Action: _____

3. On a scale of 1 to 10, rate how successful you have been in using HPI to help satisfy one of your customer's needs.

    | | Somewhat | | Very |
    | Unsuccessful | successful | | successful |
    | 1 2 3 | 4 5 6 | 7 8 | 9 10 |

4. If you scored 7 or below, begin to think about what actions you can take to more effectively satisfy your customer's needs and list them below.

    ☐ Action: _____
    ☐ Action: _____
    ☐ Action: _____

5. In the past two years, where could you have used an HPI intervention to help meet your customers' needs?

6. What prevented you from implementing an HPI intervention? What would you have done differently?

7. What do you think your organization's attitudes are toward performance improvement approaches? What actions can you take to help change any negative attitudes to positive?

    ☐ Action: _____
    ☐ Action: _____
    ☐ Action: _____

8. What is your personal assessment of HPI?

Self-Assessment 10-1.
Actions you can take to meet your customers' future performance improvement needs (continued).

9. How can you apply HPI in your business in the future?

10. What actions can you take immediately to make this happen?

☐ Action: _____

☐ Action: _____

☐ Action: _____

11

Where Do You Go From Here: Taking Charge of Your Career

 MAKE YOUR MARK IN THE TRAINING WORLD——STARTING TODAY!

It should be clear by now that for those who are experienced training professionals and for those new to the field, life ahead will be filled with challenges, opportunities, and the excitement that comes with new discoveries. This book likely will have sparked a new excitement and desire to establish your credibility in your organization and by so doing help your organization achieve its goals through the many services you provide. For every trainer, there is no better time than now for taking charge of your career.

FIFTEEN ACTIONS

Many opportunities await those enhancing their careers by becoming strategic thinkers and credible trainers; such opportunities are often a matter of looking in the right places. To help this process along, this chapter presents 15 straightforward actions for training professionals looking to further their professional development and careers starting today.

Conduct a Mini-Self-Assessment

Before you can figure out where you are going, you need to have a good understanding of where you are today and how you have arrived at that point. That is why it is important for every training professional to do a periodic self-assessment that will serve as the basis for professional and career development. To do this, take self-assessment 11-1 to evaluate where you are today and where you want to go in the future.

Read, Read, Read

With all of the books coming out every day on subjects important to trainers like leadership, management development, and performance improvement, it is almost mandatory for experienced and especially for new trainers to never go more than three weeks without starting a new book. With the advent of online bookstores, it is fairly easy to find out what books are hot sellers and read reviews on many worthwhile books. Another good resource is the information on the latest book release that comes out regularly from ASTD. Some trainers, however, make the mistake of reading only the latest literature or books on training-related subjects. Reading materials by the "old masters," such as Peter Drucker, Thomas Gilbert, Chris Argyris, and Warren Bennis, is an excellent way of gaining a perspective about where much of management, training, and business theory started. Reading books on a wide range of subjects (business, management, psychology, philosophy, and so forth) gives trainers a well-rounded education and provides them with the ability to relate better to the different audiences for their training services.

Join a Professional Organization

Because many trainers already belong to at least one of the major training organizations—ASTD, the International Society for Performance Improvement (ISPI), Society for Human Resource Management (SHRM), and others—the key here for professional development purposes is to consider taking on a leadership position by running for office, chairing a committee, or heading up a special interest group at the local chapter level.

Once you become a member, offer to conduct a presentation or program on a subject of interest to the group at a monthly meeting. Even for those trainers not yet ready or interested in taking on a position beyond simply being a member, take full advantage of every opportunity to expand your network within the group by attending meetings and other organization-sponsored events.

Do Pro Bono Work

Doing pro bono work for a nonprofit organization often ends up being a win-win proposition for both parties. For example, providing free training to a group on a subject that is of importance to them and one that you would like to develop and perhaps implement provides value to both parties. Doing pro bono work also allows you to extend your network and build a reference list for the future. Of course, every new training project you complete helps build your portfolio of services and extends your list of credentials for the future, not to mention the good feeling of providing services to those who may really need it.

Conduct a Survey

Designing and conducting a survey is an excellent professional development activity, because it allows you an opportunity to work on your writing and analytical skills. Not only that, but surveys that help determine your organization's cultural climate or uncover employee attitudes can often provide data that is useful in a variety of ways to help you achieve your company's goals. Some trainers find that conducting a survey outside their organization is an enriching professional development experience, too. For example, you can start by choosing a topic of interest in the local business community and ask, "What is the number one leadership issue facing your company today?" Next, decide on the population you are going to survey (ASTD, SHRM, or the local chamber of commerce) and contact enough people so that you get at least 30 responses. You can then publish the results in your company's newsletter, the newsletter of the organization you drew your respondents from, or even the business section of your local newspaper. Finally, send a follow-up report to all the participants and, if you like, invite them to a roundtable discussion about the topic as a way of helping build an ongoing community of learning.

Rework Your Résumé

Some may ask, "Why bother to do this if I am not looking for a job?" There are two answers to this question. First, with continual change the norm in American business today, it is important for individuals in traditionally supportive functions, such as training and development, to be able to act on the spot in the event of a reorganization, downsizing, or layoff. Perhaps, an even more important reason is that updating your résumé allows constant affirmation of what you have done in the past year and, most especially, the results that you have delivered to your customers. As you develop and grow as a training professional, your career objective inevitably changes too. Edit your résumé, keeping in mind your career objective so that you can represent more appropriately your strengths and career interests for the future.

Go on an Interview

Once again, you may be asking what is the sense of going on an interview if you are not looking for a job? This suggestion is really for those who have not been on an interview in five or more years. There are three good reasons from both a professional and career management perspective for doing this. First, it helps give you an opportunity to find out what other organizations are looking for in a training professional. This could be helpful as a means of comparing your efforts in your professional development with the kinds of experiences and expertise others in the training community are seeking. Second, it will help give you an idea of the training initiatives that other organizations are planning to implement. Third, from a very practical standpoint, it is very important to keep your interviewing skills honed. Naturally, it is important to go on an interview for a position that you may enjoy—who knows it might turn out to be something that is bigger and better than you originally imagined.

Publish

For most training professionals who have never been published, it is important to start small. Normally the biggest roadblock in taking the first step toward accomplishing this goal is the belief that no one other than you could possibly be interested in anything you have to say. This may be true for those with limited experience, because, after all, you must first build credibility if you expect others to listen to what you have to say. This is not necessarily the case, however, for more experienced trainers. Think about the successes and accomplishments you have had professionally and choose a lesson learned that you believe worth sharing with others. Case studies, "how-to" guides, and new approaches make for especially good articles. A good place to start is by writing a piece for your local ASTD chapter newsletter. If your article is not accepted the first time, ask for feedback from the publication's editor on how to improve it and either resubmit your article or choose a new subject and start again. Once you are published, start aiming your sights higher. Submit articles to ASTD's *Performance in Practice* or even a trade magazine having to do with training or the industry you work in. Contact the particular publication, ask for their publishing guidelines, write your article, and submit it. Not only is it exciting to see your name in print, it is also an excellent way to establish your credibility for the future.

Make a Video

Making an in-house video is not as farfetched as you may think. First, you need to choose a subject that warrants the time and expenditure to do one. For example, one company that had a number of offices in very remote locations decided to do information updates using a video format that they sent out to employees twice a year. The training manager was asked to coordinate the production of the videos. Because she had no experience doing this, she hired a writer and a production company to produce the videos. After the third one, she had enough experience to start writing some of the scripts and co-directing some of the episodes.

You can also incorporate videos into your training, thereby providing another excellent developmental activity and a learning tool. If you have an in-house audio-visual coordinator, discuss with him or her how to go about making a low-budget, professional-looking video that can be used to show a skill or technique in action. You can also make good use of video technology in case studies. A scenario is presented on video, and class participants are asked either to participate in role plays or decide in groups how they would resolve some of the issues raised in the case.

Become a Mentor

For trainers looking for ways to further their professional development while doing something meaningful for others, being a mentor is an opportunity to consider. Mentoring is a relationship between two people in which the mentor, using his or her experience, expertise, and knowledge, helps to enhance the mentee's personal and professional growth and development. Although some organizations have actual mentoring programs, in most cases mentoring relationships tend to be developed on a more informal basis. Trainers can choose to mentor other trainers as a way of giving something back to the training community that perhaps played an important role in their own development or choose to mentor inexperienced managers in their companies who could benefit from their guidance. From a developmental perspective, the exciting part of being a mentor is the fact that in almost every case not only does the mentee benefit, but the mentor often learns a great deal more than he or she ever expected about him- or herself.

Take a Computer Course

For those trainers who are baby boomers, the advent of computers in some ways has turned their entire lives around both professionally and personally. Unlike those whose schooling has occurred during the last 10 to 15 years, many others educated in the sixties and seventies never used a computer until they were absolutely forced to at work. Of course, today you would be hard-pressed to find any training professional who does not work on a PC or carry around a laptop. With technology changing every day, it is more critical than ever for trainers to at least have a working knowledge of some of the software and computer-based training applications that can help them better serve their customers. For those still struggling with anything beyond simple word processing, perhaps a course on how to design spreadsheets or graphics would be a good place to start. For others, learning how to make PowerPoint presentations might have more immediate application in their work. In any case, it is just not enough today to be computer literate to perform as a trainer and compete in the marketplace, you must be able to bring real value to your organization by being able to do more.

Attend a Development Workshop

Many trainers get so caught up in caring for their work that they fail to take care of themselves. Trainers should make a habit of attending at least two developmental workshops per year. These programs should include those designed to support the achievement of personal, as well as professional, development goals. Of course, many are familiar with the established programs that are offered by organizations, such as the Center for Creative Leadership, Dale Carnegie, and the American Management Association. Unfortunately, the programs offered at places like these are sometimes out of the price range of many trainers, especially those not holding the title of director or higher.

The good news is, however, that there are many less expensive programs that are offered throughout the country, which provide a good opportunity for you to attend a refresher course or to learn something new. For professional development, try choosing a program that will allow you to put into immediate action what you learn, as opposed to something strictly theory-based that you can probably find out about reading a book. Getting certified for Myers-Briggs Type Indicator (MBTI) assessments would be an example of a professional development activity that would be useful for a long time. On the personal development side, look for opportunities for inner rejuvenation through retreats or programs sponsored by nonprofit organizations where the goal is not necessarily to learn about something but to learn about yourself.

Extend Your Network

Whether you are looking to make a career move or not, the importance of networking as a means of furthering your professional development cannot be underestimated. Networking allows you the opportunity to find out what is happening in the field, the community, and the world through interactions with your colleagues and especially those you are meeting for the first time. Through networking, you can contact others who are in a position, for example, to provide consulting services to you in an area of interest to your organization. Networking also can expose you to new ideas, approaches, and methods that others in the field are using to deal with the same kinds of issues you face. Too many trainers fail to take advantage of opportunities to network with business leaders outside the field of training. These individuals are often in the best position to tell you exactly what is going on in the business world that needs fixing. Good places to network are almost limitless and include trade associations focused on HR and training (ASTD and SHRM, for example), as well as the local chamber of commerce, fraternal organizations, and volunteer organizations.

Develop Specialized Expertise

It is certainly a plus to be a well-rounded training professional, knowledgeable about and able to do many things. Being an "expert" on a particular subject, however, has its advantages, too. One trainer at a large international company took it upon himself to learn as much as he could about the study of leadership. He also took every opportunity to share what he had learned with those in his organization, as well as his colleagues on the outside. It seemed that the more he learned and spoke about it, the more his telephone rang with questions from people considering leadership development initiatives in their organizations. Not only did this trainer become the leadership "guru" in his organization, he was able to parlay his knowledge into opportunities to teach and consult with other organizations in his community—something that may pay dividends for him in the future.

Follow Your Dream

We all have dreams, but only some are courageous enough to take the risk and follow their dreams. Dreams are thoughts that creep into your mind when you find yourself saying, "Someday I'm going to . . . ." Some trainers dream of going out on their own, being their own bosses, and providing consulting services to other organizations. Others go back-and-forth about whether to go back to school for a doctorate, a master's degree, or a certificate in training and development. Still others dream of writing the book that is in all of us. Great dreams are often the precursor to greater actions. Whatever your dream, ask yourself the following questions before you take the risk:
- Does my dream truly fit into my values?
- Is my family supportive of me pursuing my dream?
- Can I financially support following my dream?
- Am I committed to making my dream come true?

If the answer to these questions is yes, then the time might just be right to follow your dream.

GRAB THE BRASS RING

No time is better than now to take action to build credibility, improve your professional development, and truly make a difference in your organization. Remember, being a successful trainer is more than using the right skills and techniques—the tactical side of the profession. It is really about thinking and acting strategically to help your organization achieve its goals. It is about using your power to influence to be a leader in helping your organization make the right decisions. Above all, it is about being someone who is honest, truthful, trusted, and competent. It is about you being a credible trainer.

Self-Assessment 11-1.
Where am I now and where am I going?

1. What do I value most personally? (List 3–5 items in ranked order.)

2. What do I value most professionally? (List 3–5 items in ranked order.)

3. Where do my personal and professional values converge? Where do they diverge?

4. What can I do to gain greater harmony between diverging values?

5. What are my three greatest professional strengths?

6. What are my three greatest professional development needs?

7. What are three actions I can take to change a developmental need to a strength?
☐ Action: _____
☐ Action: _____
☐ Action: _____

8. What are my top three personal goals?

9. What are my top three professional goals?
☐ Short-term (1–3 years) _____
☐ Mid-term (3–5 years)_____
☐ Long-term (5–10 years) _____

10. What steps must I take to ensure that I achieve each one of my goals?

11. Who can help me achieve my goals?

12. When will I know that I have achieved my goals?

References

Albrecht, K. (1994). *The Northbound Train*. New York: AMACOM.

American Society for Training & Development. (1997). 1997 National HRD Executive Survey: Trends in HRD. *1997 Third Quarter Survey Report*. Alexandria, VA: Author.

American Society for Training & Development (1998). National HRD Executive Survey. *1998 Report on Leadership Development*. Alexandria, VA: Author.

American Society for Training & Development. (1999). *State of the Industry Report*. Alexandria, VA: Author.

Bassi, L., S. Cheney, and E. Lewis. (1998, November). "Trends in Workplace Learning: Supply and Demand in Interesting Times." *Training & Development, 62*.

Bell, C. (1995, January). "The Heart of HRD Partnerships." *Training & Development, 29*.

Bennis, W., and B. Nanus. (1985). *Leaders: The Strategies for Taking Charge*. New York: Harper Perennial.

Case, J. (1995). *Open Book Management*. New York: Harper Business.

Deal, T., and A. Kennedy. (1982). *Corporate Cultures: The Rites and Rituals of Corporate Life*. Reading, MA: Addison-Wesley Publishing.

Elliott, P. (1996, December). "Power-Charging People's Performance." *Training & Development* 50(12):46–49.

Freiberg, K., and J. Freiberg. (1996). *Nuts*. Austin, TX: Bard Press.

Fuller, J., and J. Farrington. (1999). *From Training to Performance Improvement: Navigating the Transition*. San Francisco: Jossey-Bass.

Kouzes, J., and B. Posner. (1995a). *Credibility*. San Francisco: Jossey-Bass.

Kouzes, J., and B. Posner. (1995b). *The Leadership Challenge*. San Francisco: Jossey-Bass.

Levitt, T. (1986). *The Marketing Imagination*. New York: Free Press.

Robinson, D., and J. Robinson. (1995). *Performance Consulting: Moving Beyond Training*. San Francisco: Berrett-Koehler Publishers.

Rothwell, W., and D. Dubois, editors. (1998). *In Action: Improving Performance in Organizations*. Alexandria, VA: American Society for Training & Development.

Senge, P. (1990). *The Fifth Discipline*. New York: Currency Doubleday.

Stewart, T. (1997). *Intellectual Capital*. New York: Currency Doubleday.

Sugrue, B., and J. Fuller. (1999). *Performance Interventions: Selecting, Implementing, and Evaluating the Results*. Alexandria, VA: American Society for Training & Development.

Tichy, N. (1997). *The Leadership Engine*. New York: HarperCollins.

Tichy, N., and E. Cohen. (1998, July). "The Teaching Organization." *Training & Development, 27–33*.

Ulrich, D. (1996). "Credibility × Capability." In *The Leader of the Future*, F. Hesselbein, M. Goldsmith & R. Beckhard, editors. San Francisco: Jossey-Bass.

Weisbord, M. (1993). *Discovering Common Ground*. San Francisco: Berrett-Koehler Publishers.

Vaill, P. (1996). *Learning as a Way of Being*. San Francisco: Jossey-Bass.

Additional Resources

Bennis, W. (1985). *Leaders*. New York: Harper & Row.

Block, P. (1981). *Flawless Consulting*. San Diego: University Associates.

Block, P. (1993). *Stewardship*. San Francisco: Berrett-Koehler Publishers.

Boyette, J., and J. Boyette. (1998). *The Guru Guide*. New York: John Wiley & Sons.

Brinkerhoff, R., and S. Gill. (1994). *The Learning Alliance*. San Francisco: Jossey-Bass.

Case, J. (1994). *The Open Book Experience*. Reading, MA: Addison-Wesley Publishing.

Dotlich, D. and J. Noel. (1998). *Action Learning*. San Francisco: Jossey-Bass.

Goleman, D. (1998). *Working With Emotional Intelligence*. New York: Bantam Books.

Hiam, A. (1997). *Marketing for Dummies*. Foster City, CA: IDG Books Worldwide.

Robert, M. (1993). *Strategy Pure and Simple*. New York: McGraw-Hill.

Robinson, D., and J. Robinson, editors. (1998). *Moving from Training to Performance*. San Francisco: Berrett-Koehler Publishers.

Vicere, A., and R. Fulmer. (1996). *Leadership by Design*. Boston: Harvard Business School Press.

About the Author

Robert J. Rosania is a successful training and career management consultant with more than 20 years' experience working with organizations and individuals to improve performance and develop effective career management strategies. He has extensive experience in the areas of program design, development, and presentation, with an emphasis on leadership development, behavioral change, and HPI.

Rosania has a master's degree of arts in student personnel services in higher education (counseling) from Seton Hall University and bachelor's degree of arts in psychology from the University of Dayton. In addition, he has studied family therapy at Trinity Counseling Center in Princeton, New Jersey, and completed an advanced course in group leadership at the Institute for Human Relations Training in New York.

He has served as an adjunct instructor in psychology at Mercer County Community College (New Jersey) and in the leadership and motivation program at Pennsylvania State University—Ogontz. His special interest and expertise on the subject of work-life balance has led to appearances on local radio shows in Philadelphia. Rosania is an active member of ASTD and founder of the New Practitioner Special Interest Group for the greater Philadelphia chapter where he helps mentor those new to the training field. He has written articles for *Hospitals Magazine* and ASTD's *Performance in Practice* and was a featured contributor to the book *In Action: Improving Performance in Organizations* edited by William Rothwell and David Dubois (ASTD, 1998). In addition, Rosania conducts the Credible Trainer Workshop for businesses and organizations.

Rosania resides in Downingtown, Pennsylvania, with his wife, Vera Regoli, and son, Aaron. He can be reached by email at brosania@aol.com.